Sent away: a study of young offenders in care

Published in association with the Institute of Medical
Sociology, University of Aberdeen

Also published by Teakfield Limited in association with
the Institute of Medical Sociology:
A. Davis, editor, Relationships between Doctors and
        Patients, 1977

Sent away: a study of young offenders in care

J. A. WALTER

SAXON HOUSE

British Library Cataloguing in Publication Data

Walter, J A
    Sent away.
    1. Juvenile detention homes - Scotland -
Case studies
    I. Title II. University of Aberdeen. Institute
of Medical Sociology
    365'.42   HV9147.S/

✓ ISBN 0-566-00199-3

Published by

Teakfield Limited,
Westmead, Farnborough, Hants., England

ISBN 0 566 00199 3

Manufactured in England by Short Run Publishing
services. Printed and bound by Ilfadrove Limited,
Barry, Glamorgan, S. Wales

Contents

Acknowledgements

The research on which this book is based was funded
by the Social Science Research Council as part of a
programme of research at Aberdeen University. My
greatest debts here are to Professor Raymond Illsley
for the many ways in which he has sustained the
project, to David May for initiating the project and
for bearing with me in many hours of discussion, and
to Michael Lyon for painstaking work as PhD thesis
supervisor.

Intellectual support and stimulation have been
constantly available from fellow members of the SSRC
programme and from other researchers, past and present,
at the Institute of Medical Sociology. Support and
helpful comments have also come from Julius Roth, Joan
Oldman and John Geddes, and latterly from Ray Jones
and Diana Burfield. Technical assistance came from
Mike Samphier, clerical help from Pat Bruce, and
invaluable secretarial help from Jeanette Thorn and
Sheila Murray.

But my main debt by far is to the boys and staff of
Dalmore School. They did not ask to be studied for
three years, and I fear that their constant help and
giving of time have not been repaid in anything like
full measure. Sadly, such seems to be the fate of
those who let sociologists in to see life from the
inside.

Glossary

Non-Scottish readers may find this helpful.

A'	All
Bam	General derogatory term for an individual
Da'	Father
Dinna'	Don't
Fae	From
Feart	Afraid
Grass	Tell tale, sneak
Guv'	Headmaster
Halfer	Special pal with whom one goes halves
Ken	You know
Loon	Boy
Ma, Maw	Mother
Mair	More
No'	Not
O'	Of
Oot	Out
Scheme	Council housing estate
Sleekit	Sly
Sook	To curry favour with staff; one who curries favour
Square-go	A straight fight
Wis	Was

Introduction: List D schools and labelling

> 'What's the use of their having names', the
> Gnat said, 'if they won't answer to them?'
> 'No use to them', said Alice; 'but it's use-
> ful to the people that name them, I suppose.
> If not, why do things have names at all?'
> (Lewis Carroll)

How to deal with juvenile delinquency is an issue on
which there are diverging views. Restoration of law
and order is a common political slogan, but at the
same time many agencies that actually deal with young
offenders are coming to believe in a different philosophy — that offenders should not be seen as law-
breakers in need of punishment and deterrence, but as
children with social and psychological problems in
need of treatment by social workers and other
professionals.

But what do the children themselves feel? This book
tries to answer this by exploring how young offenders
sent to one residential school in Scotland are
actually processed. This school adheres to the newer
philosophy that delinquents are people with problems
in need of treatment, and so I explore how this notion
fits, or rather does not fit, in with the concerns of
the boys themselves. If, as I argue, the ideas of the
boys are as important as those of the staff, this
means that policy will be misdirected unless it takes
into account the ideas and concerns of the 'clients'
whom it is supposed to be helping.

Before proceeding, it is necessary to clarify the
plethora of titles by which residential schools for
young offenders in Britain have been named. Under
what used to be the approved school system, offenders

ix

aged from ten to seventeen could be sent by the courts
to an approved school for an indeterminate period of
between six months and three years. In April 1971,
following the Social Work (Scotland) Act 1968, the
schools in Scotland were renamed List D residential
establishments, committal to them being through the
non-judicial Children's Hearings. The equivalent act
in England and Wales was the Children and Young
Persons Act 1969, and there the schools were renamed
community homes or community schools. Since the term
'approved school' is still in colloquial use and has
the advantage of ringing some kind of bell with both
Scottish and English readers, I will use this older
term interchangeably with the new 'List D school'.

THE RESEARCH (1)

This book looks at one List D school in detail. I
spent many hours there during the years 1970-73 as a
participant observer. First I focussed on a group of
thirty-three consecutive admissions whom I attempted
to follow through the school, although contact was
also established with many other boys. This group I
refer to as 'the sample'. My observations centred on
these boys; some I took on camping and trekking exped-
itions; some wrote daily diaries for me. I interviewed them in an unstructured way within a few days
of arrival and then immediately before release, and
the release interviews were tape-recorded. I also
closely studied the files of these boys. Then in a
second phase of research I focussed on the staff. I
sat in on senior staff discussions and various other
meetings, and I interviewed all the staff except for a
few of the domestic and clerical members.

   Any scientific study rests on certain assumptions,
and it is always best to outline these. Three assumptions in particular should be mentioned here, for they
are not shared by all sociologists and criminologists
(2). They are broadly in line with what has come to
be known as labelling theory, as proposed by sociologists such as Howard Becker (1963) and David Matza

(1964; 1969).

Firstly, in any situation, especially one of conflict, the behaviour and ideas of all parties must be treated as worthy of investigation. For criminologists to find the behaviour of juvenile delinquents as requiring explanation, but not that of the agencies that deal with them, is as absurd as if the student of industry were to assume that the actions of unions but not those of management need explanation.

Secondly, society is made by men. Social categories do not just exist, they are created by people for particular purposes. Thus, delinquency is not a thing characterising certain deviant individuals, but a process by which certain people and certain actions are labelled as delinquent.

Thirdly, people are potentially conscious, thinking, feeling, purposeful beings who are not just pushed around by so-called social forces but are more or less able to influence their actions, and therefore everyone's viewpoint must be taken into account if we are to understand why people behave the way they do. If we are to understand delinquency and its treatment, we cannot automatically assume that agencies (and researchers) act purposefully and rationally, while delinquents are socially or psychologically determined.

Thus this book looks at both sides - at the staff and the boys in the school. It views both as actively defining their situation - the boys as very much concerned with certain things and acting to meet these concerns, and the staff as actively trying to implement their ideas of treatment. I particularly look at the way in which staff label the boys, and how these labels relate to both the staff's ideas and to the boys' concerns.

OUTLINE OF THE BOOK

Chapter 1 introduces the school studied, 'Dalmore',

and Chapter 2 examines the view of the school held by
the senior staff, a view which tends towards a treatment model of delinquency. According to this view, or
'official philosophy', boys who get into trouble do
not need punishment, nor do they primarily need
discipline and a new set of values; rather, each boy
has got into trouble because of individual 'problems'
he faces at home, at school or elsewhere in the
community. These are the root cause of his behaviour,
and his delinquency is merely a symptom. In this view
the task of Dalmore is to help the boy to face up to
his 'problems' and if possible to try to remove the
'problems' altogether. 'Individual treatment' for
each boy is the key phrase of this official philosophy.

This view is not completely accepted by all levels
of staff, but those staff who are less in sympathy are
those who have little direct influence on treatment
decisions about boys and whose work situation is not
conducive to their working out a cohesive counter-
philosophy. Consequently, while the official philosophy becomes more shared, the views of those who are
not in sympathy are becoming more fragmented.

Chapter 3 looks at Dalmore from the boys' view. If
the official philosophy is concerned with the personal
'problems' that caused each boy to get into trouble,
the boys have a rather different set of immediate
concerns. Getting into trouble is something which has
happened to them and they are not concerned to dig
down into their past to see how they got into trouble;
rather, they want to know how to get out of trouble.
Trouble for them at the moment means being in a
residential school, so they are concerned to get out
of Dalmore. They assume that what is required is not
insight into and discussion of their 'emotional
problems' but good behaviour (3). Behaving is not
always easy though as it can always be defined by
other boys as 'sooking' and consequent lack of popul-
arity may be feared, and so, as well as getting out,
behaving well becomes a second main concern. Boys are
concerned, also, about getting on with each other;
they have been told over the years that places like

Dalmore are the end of the road for bad boys and so
they fear, on committal, what kind of boys the others
will be. They are also concerned about maintaining a
certain level of comfort, even though they are
relatively well off compared to the inmates of some
other institutions. They are concerned about how to
have fun and enjoy themselves in a situation where
they are under a lot more adult supervision than they
are used to.

The boys' immediate concerns then are different from
those of senior staff. Senior staff say that what is
important are problems that exist or originate outside
and prior to committal to Dalmore, whereas the boys
are most immediately concerned with difficulties that
are inside and the result of being in Dalmore. For
them Dalmore is not the solution to being in trouble,
it constitutes trouble.

How then do the boys' view and the official philosophy confront each other? This question is answered
in Part Two by looking at the ways in which senior
staff actually go about formulating the 'problems' of
individual boys.

Chapter 4 looks at what is for staff the most readily
available source of information about life outside,
namely the boy himself. But the boys do not usually
see it as important to talk about problems outside
and, even when they do, they see talking about them to
be more likely to delay then speed up release.

There are various structured situations designed to
facilitate boys talking about their 'problems', such
as group counselling, interviews with social work
staff, and more general conversations with other staff.
However, although these situations permit the boys to
talk about personal problems, there is little in any
of these situations which requires boys to talk in
this way. Thus, many boys arrive at release not having
talked in this way to any member of staff.

Since the official philosophy sees the boys' problems

to be located outside or to originate outside Dalmore,
Chapter 5 looks at information arriving from outside.
This consists largely of the social enquiry reports
that accompany each boy to a List D school, of subsequent contacts from the local social work department, and of contacts from his parents. In each case,
there is not routinely available the kind of information needed to formulate a boy's problems. In the
case of parental contacts, this is because the parents
tend to have a model of delinquency that is different
from the models both of their children and of Dalmore
staff.

In Chapter 6 the criteria for deciding that boys are
ready for release are examined. It is found that
achieving a solution to their individual problems is
not a prime consideration, and that the routine grounds
for releasing boys have to do with their good behaviour
and with the chance facts of their age and of the
school leaving dates in their local education authorities. Since getting released is the boys' major
concern, these grounds on which release is decided -
fate and good behaviour - are highly influential in
confirming their view of what Dalmore is all about.

In Chapter 7, I draw several threads together and
discuss how the official philosophy and the boys' view
remain tenable to each side. Important factors here
are the peculiar flexibility and ambiguity of the
language of the treatment philosophy, and the
situations in which it is propounded. The book
concludes with a discussion of an unexpected con-
vergence between staff and boys in the way they
explain deviance and this is related to a general
consideration of how people come to want explanations
of social behaviour in everyday life.

NOTES

(1) A full account of the research project and its
findings may be found in Walter (1975a).
(2) For critiques of other studies of approved schools

see Walter (1977) and Taylor (1971).
(3) Throughout the book, the term 'behaviour' refers
to the layman's use of the term which implies a
judgement - to behave oneself means to behave well.
The more recent notion held by scientists and social
scientists of 'behaviour' as ethically neutral is not
intended here.

PART I

STAFF AND BOYS

1   Dalmore

Of course, the first thing to do was to make a
grand survey of the country she was going to
travel through.   (Lewis Carroll)

Commitment to a List D school is through the
Children's Hearings, a sitting of a lay body called
the Children's Panel which is the channel for
formally dealing with most juvenile offenders. The
child then usually goes to an assessment centre
(formerly a remand home) while a place at a List D
school is arranged via the central administrative
machinery of the Social Work Services Group in
Edinburgh. Once at a school, the child is the day-to-
day responsibility of the school, but his release
(often called 'licence') may only be authorised by the
Children's Hearing. A Hearing to review his case, a
'Review Hearing', must be held within a year, although
the child or his parents may request a review after
three months and thereafter at six-monthly intervals.
The official who channels children to the Children's
Hearing is called the Reporter (1).

There are nineteen List D schools for boys in Scotland (2). The system is divided by age into junior
(age on admission up to thirteen), intermediate
(thirteen to fifteen), and senior schools (fifteen to
seventeen). This means that junior schools tend to
consist of boys all under school leaving age, senior
schools of boys all over school leaving age, and
intermediate schools a mixture. Education is provided
on the premises for those legally requiring it and
some form of work or trade training for the older boys.
In August 1972, however, the school leaving age was
raised from fifteen to sixteen which decimated the
number of intermediate boys who were over school
leaving age. As will be seen in later chapters, the
effect of this on the boys in the school was possibly

3

greater than the changes wrought by the Social Work (Scotland) Act.

THE SCHOOL

Dalmore is a local authority-managed school accommodating about a hundred boys. Possibly its main measurable distinguishing feature is that the nine-month average length of stay is about half that of the seventeen-month average of most other intermediate schools (HMSO 1972). Weekend home leave is once a fortnight and often once a week.

There is no wall round the school and there is physically nothing to stop a boy walking out of the school: absconding is seen by boys more as walking out than running away. By no means all doors are locked all the time and when a door is locked it is locked more to keep boys out of areas of the school not covered by staff supervision rather than to keep them in the school buildings themselves. However, the possession by staff of keys makes mobility around the school considerably easier for them than for boys and is a symbol of the basic lack of freedom of the boys.

A short way from the main building is 'the Cottage' - a newer unit accommodating up to thirty boys, often the weakest, youngest or most 'disturbed'. The furnishings here are new and ample and the atmosphere is more reminiscent of a student hostel than of a school. Apart from the Cottage, the school is divided into houses but this is for little more than administrative purposes. There are no house prefects, nor is there any official hierarchy for boys within a house. Each house has three or four staff attached to it; the name 'housemaster' sometimes refers to any of these but is increasingly reserved for the senior man in each house, who now is a qualified residential social worker. Thus every boy has a social worker in Dalmore who is responsible for him, in addition to a social worker from the Social Work Department in his home town. I will use the terms 'housemaster' or 'social worker' to

4

refer to the Dalmore man, unless the context is ambiguous in which case I will call him the Dalmore or school social worker. The man in the field, in the boy's home town, will be called a field or local social worker.

Boys are allowed to smoke, but not to keep their own tobacco. This is bought weekly for each boy, and enough for one roll-up is handed out six times a day. This is intended to eliminate the system of tobacco barons common in many institutions.

Each boy has a number in the range 1-100 which is mainly used for identifying his clothing and his tobacco tin. Usually staff address him by his Christian name or a nickname derived from his surname. This often comes as a mild surprise to the new boy who expects to be addressed by his surname and it may emphasise to him that the staff are attempting a relationship more reminiscent of social work than of school or of dealings with the police. Surnames are sometimes used when staff wish to be angry, and in routine roll calls. The boy's number is not nearly as much a part of his identity as is the case in prisons and it would be unfair to say that at Dalmore the boy is a number; rather he has a number.

The visitor's first impression of Dalmore is likely to be one of informality and a level of spontaneity not expected in such institutions. This relaxed atmosphere though is periodically broken by incongruous shouting by staff or lining up of boys reminiscent of a more disciplinarian regime.

THE BOYS

Most of the boys are committed to Dalmore following theft of some kind. As they are committed by a non-judicial body, the Children's Hearing, there are no statistics available on the original offences, but probably committals to Dalmore are distributed similarly to the national figures for England and

Wales (HMSO 1972:2).

The size and nature of the populations of boys' and girls' approved schools are very different. For example, in Scottish schools on March 31st, 1969 (HMSO 1970), there were eleven times as many boys as girls, and whereas almost all the boys were committed for offences, rather over half of the girls were committed as being 'in need of care and protection'.

The average number of previous court appearances for Dalmore boys is of the order of three and about a quarter have been in approved school before.

The boys come predominantly from social classes 3, 4 and 5. They come from all over Scotland, and most live in or near the four major cities of Glasgow, Edinburgh, Dundee and Aberdeen. Apart from age, there is no formal way in which the intake at Dalmore is specialised.

Concerning education and IQ ratings, the boys differ little from the national picture in 1962 as presented by Field et al. (1971:42). Educational attainment, as measured by reading age, is on average some years behind chronological age, even though the average IQ is only slightly below 100. The range of IQ is wide. Although most are in the 80-100 range, there is usually at least one boy who is arguably in the 60's and one boy I knew was measured at 136. During the research no boys took GCE or CSE exams.

The age range of the boys (13-16) seems narrow but I was constantly struck by the contrast between the childlike nature of some of the younger boys and the adultness of some of the older boys. Within the space of a few minutes I could play toy tractors on the floor with one boy and then talk to another soon to become a father.

THE STAFF

The number of staff has expanded considerably in
recent years, and as with other List D schools it is
the social work sector that is the most rapidly expand-
ing. The staff are largely native to the local area,
the three most recent exceptions being the headmaster
together with two social workers who followed in his
footsteps from his previous school. Apart from a few
domestic and secretarial staff, all the staff are aged
over thirty.

The staff are predominantly lower middle class and
upwardly mobile working class, and this seems to be
typical of approved schools (Jones 1965). The working
class affiliation of many of the staff and the manual
nature of some of their work means that their social
class is much nearer that of the boys than is common
in several allied professions such as social work and
teaching. For some staff, however, Dalmore comprises
an introduction to, and ladder into, the lower middle
class; for example, a gardener or a janitor may live
in one of the school houses in a distinctly respectable area of town. Such upwardly mobile staff often
show values which have more in common with their class
of arrival than the class of departure. Pay is better
than in comparable jobs outside; for example, a
Dalmore teacher earns a good 25 per cent more than his
equivalent in a normal secondary school. Instructors
may or may not earn more than equivalent tradesmen
outside, depending on the state of their trade, but
job security at Dalmore compensates for any reduction
in pay.

None of the staff have been in approved school work
all their working lives and none chose such work as a
career before completing their formal education in the
way that many young undergraduates today have chosen
social work as a career. Tutt's (1974:101) study of a
similar school refers to:

> ....the haphazard way in which each of them
> 'drifted' into child care, in most cases with

very little knowledge of what the work was about.

As Tutt points out, though, this does not mean that they are any less committed to their work than those who have chosen a career.

I will now briefly describe each of the major grades of staff and the nature of their work:

Domestic staff

The daily task of the domestic staff is to keep the boys clothed and fed. To help in this a small number of boys are allocated to them each day to perform menial work such as laying tables and running messages. Some boys may be allocated on a part-time basis because it is felt they are not profitting from attending classes or that they need a bit of mothering. Boys over school leaving age who show no particular pref- erence for any of the trade instruction groups may form a residual category which gets allocated to these more menial tasks.

Trade instructors

The instructors are all qualified tradesmen, some of whom have also had teaching experience. They perceive their work to consist of several tasks, some men emphasising some aspects more than others: 1) to teach good work habits; 2) to teach specific skills; 3) social education, such as fostering self-confidence, a pride in work, and discipline; 4) to maintain and extend the fabric of the school; 5) to counsel the boys and build up a constructive relationship with them. In addition to these tasks, the instructor also has to: 6) maintain enough order to get on with whatever task is on hand; 7) cope with frequent changes in the squad of boys allocated to him.

These various tasks are often conflicting, a situat- ion common to other approved schools (Tutt 1974:192- 93). The requirement to keep the fabric in good order often leads to working under pressure that does not

allow time to teach boys specific skills. Teaching
technical skills to a small squad of boys and giving
time to discussing the personal problems of individual
boys may not both be possible.

Given the impossibility of the simultaneous fulfilment of all their tasks, there is a tendency for
instructors to restrict their job to either the teaching of trade skills or the more interpersonal social
work aspects. Some instructors are happy to remain as
instructors while others, having had contact with
social work in Dalmore, begin to aspire to a year's
training course in residential child care and promotion
to a new career in social work.

However, all instructors feel they have become something in addition to tradesmen, that they have become
part of 'the approved school service'. Although this
is not so clearly delineated an occupation as, say,
the prison service or the army, there is an identity
associated with working in a List D school such that
increasingly one identifies with staff in other List D
schools and possibly decreasingly with other, say,
joiners or plumbers in the trade outside. This possibly helps account for the low rate of return to their
trade among the well-established; they are now
engaged in 'approved school work' and to return to
being a joiner or a plumber would indicate failure,
whereas this would be less marked if a domestic left
or a teacher returned to non-residential teaching.

Classroom teachers

The teachers all have previous experience in secondary
schools. Their work in Dalmore is different from
their previous work in that they have small classes;
with a total roll per class of between eight and
twenty, the number of pupils actually in the classroom
at any one time may be considerably less. Teaching is
usually on an individual basis of each child progressing at his own rate; this is facilitated by small
classes and is also necessary if boys are to be free
to leave the classroom at short notice to go to school

9

meetings or to see the headmaster or social work staff.

Controlling pupils in class is easier than in ordinary secondary schools. This is partly because of the small class size and the opportunity this presents for the teacher to get to know each boy well enough to be able to handle him, and also because those nearing school leaving age - the 'early leavers' who are seen to cause so much bother by secondary school teachers - may be siphoned off slightly before the legal age into work groups. But possibly most importantly the Dalmore teacher has ultimate sanctions that his secondary school counterpart has not - the ability to cancel home leave, possibly to delay release, and the threat of what is for many boys the ultimate sanction of transfer to another List D school entailing a harsher regime and a longer stay.

Social workers

There were by the end of the research, seven social workers, one being the third-in-charge, one for each of the three school houses, one for each of the two Cottage houses, and one spare. Four of these had been trade instructors and had gone on a year's residential child care course to qualify as social workers. Each has general oversight of each of the fifteen or so boys in his house. This low caseload, together with their upper working class background, late entry into social work, and the fact they are all male, means that their work and their approach to it is different from those of field social workers.

The orientation and work of the social workers in many ways is also different from the teachers. Because of their social and educational background, the social workers may identify more with the instructors than with the teachers. Also, teachers have traditionally dominated approved schools and almost without exception headmasters have been teachers by profession. But social work is now challenging this supremacy in both the philosophy of the schools and in the composition of the middle and upper levels of staff (Millham et al.

10

1973:13).

The social worker's day is more varied than that of
any of the previous types of staff mentioned. A large
proportion of his time is spent contacting people who
affect the passage of his fifteen boys through Dalmore,
and he does much of the arranging for their admission,
leave and release. The social worker talks with the
newly admitted boy to discuss Dalmore and to glean
information from him about his family and friends in
order to supplement the outside social worker's social
enquiry report. He arranges the return of a boy if he
absconds. He reads incoming mail before passing it on
to the boy. He is in correspondence with the Reporter
to the Children's Panel if it is time for a boy to be
licensed or if he has been apprehended by the police
for some offence while on leave. He writes reports on
the boy's progress in school and on what he knows of
the family situation for the Children's Hearing if a
boy is to go there for a review with a view to release
or for having committed an offence, and he may travel
to a Children's Hearing to give the report. He
receives visiting social workers who come to deliver a
new admission or who have just dropped in because they
are passing by and have a boy in Dalmore.

The headmaster

The headmaster spends most of the day in the Board
Room. This is dominated by a large polished table
around which up to fifteen people can sit, and this
table symbolises that the room is less a headmaster's
office than a decision-making centre in which decisions
can be made on a group basis. The headmaster's day is
varied: reading mail, dictating replies, talking to
staff and boys who call or are called in to see him,
seeing parents, answering the phone, assimilating news
from outside about the reorganisation of Social Work
in Scotland and passing it on to staff, arranging mod-
ifications to the school buildings, chairing meetings
in the school, and receiving visiting social workers,
students and others. He may be called out of the
Board Room to settle some trouble between staff and

boys, or he may go to see a member of staff. Occasionally he goes to speak about the school to outside audiences of a professional or academic kind.

In any List D school the headmaster is in a position of power. He is the only member of staff present at meetings of the Board of Governors, and although he is theoretically appointed to run the school under and as directed by the managers, the managers are dependent on him for information about the school (Jones 1965: 103-4) and he is the one who interprets Board decisions to his staff. He has further power vis-a-vis his staff; he effectively hires and fires them and, insofar as many staff dwell in school houses, the power to fire entails the power to evict (Tutt 1974:153).

At Dalmore the headmaster is very much at the centre of things, and he could be described as a charismatic leader. Personal charisma develops when someone can furnish services for another such that they feel personally indebted to him (Blau 1963). If those services are in the interests of a group of people rather than of an individual then a group norm legitimating his authority may emerge, even for those who have not yet received any such services. This has largely happened through the provision of new classrooms, workshops and other facilities and many staff express their loyalty to the headmaster in terms of such material improvements. Boys feel indebted because the provision of frequent leave, a short average length of stay and other comforts are usually attributed to the personal beneficience of the headmaster. But the staff group most indebted are the social workers, i.e. those who have been brought in to senior positions by the headmaster from their previous school or have been enabled to take a year off in order to qualify for promotion from instructor to social worker. I will now look in a little more detail at the way in which the social workers are now at the centre of things and the way in which teachers, instructors and domestics feel increasingly powerless.

POWER AMONG THE STAFF

One member of staff referred to a 'board room clique' consisting of the headmaster, deputy, social workers and senior teacher, with the two Cottage housefathers incorporated for formal gatherings of the group. The designation of these men to such a group is a little arbitrary, and core and peripheral members could be identified slightly differently.

    Core –   headmaster, deputy, two chief social workers

    Periphery – other social workers, Cottage housefathers and senior teacher

Apart from students, these men are the only people to be found regularly sitting in the Board Room, the place where almost all major decisions affecting the school or individual boys are made. Further, it is these men who regularly attend, and who have a timetable that allows them to attend, meetings at which the boys are assessed. I will subsequently refer to this group as 'senior staff', or as 'the social work staff' since, although one or two members are not social workers, the ethos of the group is dominated by social work concepts.

The lack of being in at the centre of things for all the other staff has several consequences. They don't know for certain exactly when anything is going to happen so even if they are free to be present they may well miss it. Also, information about decisions regarding boys or antics they have been up to tends to get relayed through coffee-room talk and other highly arbitrary channels. A typical incident occurred while I was interviewing one junior female member of staff in the staff dining-room; at one point a social worker came in looking for the deputy head. She asked him about a boy who'd been to court last week and the social worker then spent five minutes or so describing the details of the offence and the complicated legal proceedings. It was thus only chance that she heard

13

the news that was already a week old.

Those who are not in the senior staff group may have difficulty knowing how to approach the headmaster. His door is officially always open but is in fact often closed so they don't know the best time to visit the Board Room; and their bargaining position with the headmaster is weakened by their lack of up-to-date information and by lack of experience in negotiating with him. This is in marked contrast to senior staff who regularly observe the head negotiating with every-one from the youngest boy to those who pull the nat-ional purse strings. As one of the senior staff - a Cottage housefather - said to me:

> I can go down to the Board Room and I can argue
> with the headmaster and push my case. And if
> he doesn't budge then I just carry on arguing
> and often as not I might persuade him....I would
> like to think the headmaster depended on me for
> knowledge about a boy and recommendations and
> this kind of thing.

Compare this with the comment of a rather dissatisfied instructor about one of the social workers:

> He knows how to please the headmaster. He's
> been sitting there in the Board Room for six
> years. So he knows when to agree with the
> headmaster and when to disagree....And of
> course he can even be angry at him because
> he knows the right time.

Another instructor complained to me that those who were not social workers had been eased out of the monthly assessment meeting:

> To be quite frank, I'm never consulted. I'm just
> asked for the odd report occasionally. Before
> we can have a proper grading system it's got
> to be not just the social workers sitting round.
> Mind, it's difficult to say we should have all
> the staff meeting every month because there's

too many boys to go through. But I think we
should have something like that. Then there
would be a better discussion on each boy. You
know, I've not been asked for a report for
months. So how do the social workers know
what's going on with a boy? They don't see
every boy. So a boy may go up a grade when it's
the wrong decision.

Every non-domestic, non-secretarial member of staff
is attached to a house. However, the role that non-
social work staff play within the house has been
declining, partly in order to let the tradesmen get on
with the rebuilding of much of the school. Some men
are resentful of this loss of influence over the boys,
others are content to see themselves being reduced from
housemasters to tradesmen. More important in their
eyes, though, is their loss of disciplinary powers.
They know that the boys know that the power to stop
home leave or to delay release lies not in their hands
but in the hands of the headmaster and social workers.

The only basis for most staff's authority over the
boys, apart from their technical expertise as a joiner,
cook or whatever, is personal charisma - this is in
accord with the situation in so-called 'therapeutic
communities' where staff are supposed to build up
authority through personal interaction with inmates
(e.g. Wills 1971:150-51). Blau's analysis of authority
derived from the gratuitous provision of services
clearly fits the headmaster and to some extent the
social workers as these men provide boys with the
'service' of release and home leave, but the other
staff are not empowered to grant release or leave and
consequently they feel singularly without personal
authority. The loss of influence over a boy's fate
makes discipline more difficult for instructors and
junior staff.

The raising of the school leaving age in 1973 further
reduced the power of instructors and domestic staff.
Before then, about a quarter of the boys were over
school leaving age and worked for days or weeks on end

15

with one instructor or with domestic staff. Consequently these staff got to know a few boys very well and were consulted for their views on them and were requested to write reports on them. Now, however, almost all boys are rotating round the various workshops such that instructors and domestics have little chance through the day-time to develop relations with even a few boys. Teachers, however, are now of more importance since the task of fitting boys to return to secondary school is of high priority and the work of the classroom is now more highly valued.

The loss of influence following the raising of the school leaving age possibly most strongly affects kitchen staff and tailoring staff who are now less dependent on help from boys in the running of their areas. One of the kitchen staff referred in interview to the male staff as 'officials', almost as though she saw herself as an 'unofficial', i.e. not really a proper member of staff. Tutt (1974:166) noted a similar situation in the school he studied:

> Neither (the boys or the professional staff) view the domestic staff as really staff.... The professional staff exclude the domestic staff from certain staff activities. They do not attend...staff meetings, case conferences or in-service teaching schemes.

To conclude, then, those staff who have most day-to-day contact with boys - teachers, instructors and domestic staff - have less say in the running of the school and in deciding the careers of boys through the school than do the social workers and other senior staff. The increasing professionalisation and influence of the social workers is in line with national trends, and it is these staff who are in closest day-to-day contact with the headmaster who is the chief decision-maker and definer of the nature of work at Dalmore. In the next chapter I will look in more detail at how the headmaster and senior staff actually set about defining their work.

NOTES

(1) An introduction to this system may be found in Social Work Services Group (1976).
(2) See Scottish Education Dept. (1976).

2   The official philosophy

Then a very gentle voice said, 'She must be
labelled "Lass, with care", you know......'
(Lewis Carroll)

There are many and conflicting views about juvenile
delinquency, views often associated with the numerous
professional personnel concerned with dealing with it
- magistrates, police, teachers, social workers, psy-
chiatrists, and so on. Textbooks on criminology and
penology also display a bewildering variety of views.
In this chapter I look at the dominant views that
Dalmore staff hold about delinquency and how to deal
with it. I refer to this shared set of views as
Dalmore's 'official philosophy' (Strauss et al. 1964).

The word 'philosophy' is one that is used by the
headmaster for the collective set of his ideas, and
other people recognise him and to some extent the
school as holding a philosophy. The academic reader,
however, should beware imposing on this term an over-
emphasis on rationality, internal logical coherence, or
deduction from abstract principles. As Gittins (1966:
49) and Carlebach (1970:54) have pointed out, most
approved school staff work out their philosophy in an
ad hoc manner over the years by reflecting on their
own experience of working with delinquent boys, not by
logical deduction from a grand theoretical system.

To talk of a Dalmore philosophy as a shared or collective set of ideas does not necessarily mean that
anything like all staff at the school subscribe to all
aspects of the philosophy. Indeed, I will argue that
the official philosophy at Dalmore is only articulated
regularly and publicly by the relatively small number
of senior staff, but these men have such a degree of
control over the structure and functioning of the
school that their philosophy may be designated the

18

'official' or 'dominant' philosophy, even 'the Dalmore philosophy'. Other philosophies, because unofficial, are articulated publicly less often and consequently become increasingly discrete ideas held by individuals rather than shared sets of ideas that could be designated a 'philosophy'.

The official philosophy at Dalmore is articulated in an evangelical style. One of the most immediately noticeable features of the school is that the headmaster and social workers actively propagate their views, their main audiences being visitors (including researchers) and the boys. These audiences are often presumed to hold more traditional views on the purpose of List D schools, and so it is felt active evangelism is necessary. With boys this takes place when a social worker explains to the new boy how the school is run. Visitors to the school are varied and include Children's Panel members, trainee teachers and social workers, field social workers visiting one of the boys, colleagues from other residential establishments, researchers from universities or the Scottish Home and Health Department, and youth clubs and women's guilds. Time permitting, there is usually a correlation between the professional status of the visitors and whether or not they are seen by the headmaster - whereas a women's guild may be shown round the school by a social worker, Children's Panel members are likely to spend a substantial time in the Board Room discussing with the headmaster the philosophy and running of the school or of the Children's Hearings.

Evangelism is not the only purpose of articulating the philosophy to visitors and boys. These audiences are also seen as sounding boards whose response may be used in the ongoing process of working out the philosophy. Thus, these situations consist not so much of a pre-packed lecture as a throwing out of ideas in order to initiate some kind of dialogue and a means by which senior staff can interpret and reflect on what kind of work they are engaged in. Practice and philosophy are related in a continuous two-way process in which philosophy is derived from an interpretation of

practice and in which practice is derived from an
interpretation of philosophy.

FROM TRAINING TO TREATMENT

Among the old approved schools and the new List D
schools and community homes there is a wide range of
philosophies, but there does seem to be a definite
shift away from talk about <u>training</u> children, meaning
desocialising them out of their old ways and resocialising them into a new set of values by means of a firm
and consistent (but not necessarily harsh) regime.
(See HMSO 1937, Simmons 1946 and Adam 1964 for esp-
ousals of the training model). Now the tendency is to
talk in terms of treatment (1). This trend has been
officially embodied in recent reports and in the legislation that has turned approved schools into 'community
schools and homes' in England and into 'List D establishments' in Scotland (HMSO 1964, 1968b, 1968c).
This legislation unquestioningly accepts a 'treatment'
model of delinquency and the corresponding medical
terminology such as 'cure', 'symptom', 'diagnosis'
(May 1972). The English White Paper, 'Children in
Trouble' (HMSO 1968a:11) begins its section on residential treatment by omitting all reference to the old
type of 'training' establishment:

> The abolition of the approved school order means
> that children and young persons who would now be
> committed to approved schools will come into the
> care of the local authority in whose area they
> live. The basic duty of local authorities towards
> children in their care will remain that of
> providing the care, protection, guidance or
> treatment which they consider appropriate in the
> interests of each child.

And (p.12):

> There will be a continuing need for some estab-
> lishments providing education and treatment on
> the premises....Some of these children, partic-

20

ularly those whose behaviour is most difficult,
will also need control in secure conditions, or
very specialised forms of treatment.

The increasing call for 'treatment' based on a medical
model to replace 'training' has also been noted by
Rose (1967), Carlebach (1970) and Jones (1968). But
does this trend involve a change in regimes or a change
in philosophy or in what? Is it just becoming fashion-
able to talk of 'treatment' rather than 'training'
irrespective of whether there has actually been any
change in what goes on in the schools? Whatever the
answers, one thing is certain - the rhetoric is
changing, even if it is ambiguous or involves merely
a change in words without a change in concepts.

   Where does Dalmore stand in relation to all this?
In the rest of this chapter I hope to show that its
philosophy fits the treatment model more closely than
the other models. Senior Dalmore staff often claim to
professional outsiders that theirs is the most forward-
thinking List D school in Scotland and that they are
several years in advance of other schools, and the
language of the treatment model recurs frequently.

MAIN THEMES OF THE OFFICIAL PHILOSOPHY

I will describe the main themes of the philosophy under
the headings of the causes of delinquency and the
regime of individual treatment.

1. *The causes of delinquency*

A strictly retributive establishment is not concerned
with the causes of crime. If, however, reform or
treatment is the goal, then some attention will be paid
to the cause of a person's offending as well as to the
offending itself. The more treatment-oriented the
establishment, the more important 'causes' become:

   I don't attach too much importance to the offence.
   I'm concerned with children. If you work in a

21

school of this kind you find that the children
come here for all kinds of things - rape,
attempted murder, not attending school. The
whole thing is ludicrous if you look at it from
the point of view of the offence. But if you
accept that these are children who are deprived,
are in need of care, in need of help, then you
can't help after a time recognising that for
ninety-nine per cent of the time - oh, more than
that - these boys are really first-rate citizens...
We recognise that they are children who have
committed offences against society, and for that
reason have to be taken away. But having accepted
that, our main concern is with the fact that they
are children, and that they do not become delinquents. I do not see them as delinquent and
I can't do anything other than concern myself
with the child rather than the offence.
(headmaster)

The constant reference to 'children' rather than
'delinquents' implies a commitment to their whole personality rather than to their offending activities;
that is, a commitment to treatment of the individual
rather than to correction of his offending. A further
implication is that the reasons why a child has got
into trouble are a central concern.

   In Dalmore's view, the cause of boys getting into
trouble is other people. Explanations of criminality
in terms of the evil nature of the individual are
rejected, as are biological/hereditary explations,
except as a very rarely used residual category for
behaviour that is so bizarre that no other explanation
is available. Getting into trouble is seen as a result
of abnormal psychological development or of an abnormal
socio-economic-cultural environment. Basically the
trouble is other people, especially adults:

   I think that most children get here because
   people don't understand their needs and that's
   from the parents, teachers, social workers,
   people in children's homes, you name it. There

22

is very little real understanding.

I think practically all of the breakdown in
children can be traced to bad handling by adults.
Now bad handling may mean sending a child away
when he shouldn't be sent away, that's bad
handling and it certainly will mean after he's
sent away not understanding the needs of the
child. I think that it starts first of all in
the home and then it progresses...............
(headmaster)

The other people who cause the trouble fall into
several groups:

The family: A dominant theme of the official philosophy
is that whoever else subsequently may be to blame for
a child being in difficulties, it all starts in the
home. This identification of 'family pathology' as the
seed-bed of delinquency is by no means peculiar to
Dalmore. It is thoroughly typical of the view of List
D and community schools staff and related practitioners
throughout the country, and documentation of this is
legion, e.g. Rose (1967:54), Gill (1974:37), Tutt
(1974:9-15), Mason (1968:18-20), Miller (1968:75). It
is also in line with government reports (e.g. Home
Office Advisory Council on Child Care 1970) and with
the recent reorganisation of local authority social
work around the family as the basic unit. Also, most
academic criminology stresses family pathology as the
cause of delinquency, as does the psychoanalytic trad-
ition.

The explanations of delinquency offered at Dalmore
are often subtle, complex and eclectic. It is rarely
if ever claimed that the family is always the cause
or the only cause of delinquency. Also, the interpretation by the boy himself of his family situation
is often emphasised and explanations that incorporate
this are not necessarily deterministic nor are they a
crude amassing of statistically significant pathogenic
factors. This is illustrated briefly in the following
analysis by the headmaster of the situation of many

boys on being released home:

> Then he comes home and he becomes just as irrit-
> ating because his parents are irritating him,
> and, you know, it's just the whole thing of
> living together, and he's forced out into the
> streets. And he finds himself without work, with
> kindred spirits, penniless, he gets that kind of
> harmful talk that some fellows are noted for -
> the kind of talk that in fact forces boys, even
> against their will, through bravado or what have
> you, to do things they wouldn't otherwise do.

Here the argument is eclectic and emphasises subcultural pressures as much as anything, but crucially
the boy would never get into such a subculture were
things all right at home. This is typical of the way
almost any sociological theory of delinquency can be
postulated without challenging the assumption that at
the base of it all may lie an unhappy home.

This assumption was made, for example, by social work
staff when they told me how they go about their first
in-depth interview with a boy. The boy's family is the
most important thing they want to know about:

> Really the statement on the form that the boy's
> committed an offence of, say, housebreaking and
> the story I get told by the boy are two completely
> different things and so I'd go on to ask about
> the boy's parents, how he got on with his brothers
> and sisters.....

I asked another social worker what he would ask the
field social worker who escorts a new boy to the
school? He emphasised:

> I try to get as much information on the home back-
> ground as possible, what the social worker feels
> has caused the breakdown, and I'd go through the
> file and have a quick squint at, say, the medical
> reports to see if the child has been in hospital
> for a long time (i.e. parental deprivation) or

24

some upheaval at home.

A housefather in the Cottage told me that when a boy came up to the Cottage he'd get hold of the file straight away; I asked him what in the file he would look out for:

> Well, for example, who the parents are. If the father is away from home. What name the mother calls herself by. If the boy is illegitimate. Basically, it's about the family.

And during the next week or so he would look out for:

> His contact with the home. Does he get letters? Does he write letters? Is he going on leave?...

Two particular social workers are especially keen on psychoanalytic theories emphasising the family. In their view, characteristics of a boy such as bed-wetting, over-eating and sleeping habits are all symptomatic of anxiety about the mother. These social workers showed such enthusiasm over this approach that they recommended books to me on the subject.

So far the illustrative material on the family has come from the headmaster and five of the seven social workers, and the other two social workers are no exception to this pattern. All of them see the family as either the area in which to seek explanations for why their boys are in trouble, or as the root cause underlying other explanations (to do with school, sub-cultures, etc.). The many and varied criticisms by these men of local authority social work departments often concern their failure to work with families. There is deep feeling that without such work with families all the efforts of the Dalmore staff may be in vain:

> I can't ensure that there's jobs for them, to keep them off the streets, and to give them the chance to develop further, I can't change the parents - I can do nothing on that side, I can

only try to make social work departments or social
workers see what the problem is. At the end of
the day I am not doing a very good job.
(headmaster)

The school: The way in which the family is seen as
dominant in the explanation of delinquency is shown in
the following analysis of the Dalmore population
presented by the headmaster in a lecture to under-
graduate psychology students. It also indicates how
schooling is seen as the next most important area:

> 52 from broken homes
> 12 fostered
> 10 had step-parents
> 2 had parents of foreign extract which caused
>   difficulty
> 6 father cohabiting
> 9 mothers known to be cohabiting
> 6 fathers were regular soldiers
> 25 reported to have a poor father relationship
>   and I think that's an under-estimate
> Almost all had run away from home at some point
> 67 truanted
> 5 committed to Dalmore for truancy
> 26 had been to child guidance clinics
> 12 had been given outpatient psychiatric treatment
> 4 had been given inpatient psychiatric treatment

If the trouble starts in the home, school is seen as
the most likely first stumbling block for the child.
To continue a previous quote from the headmaster:

> ...It starts first of all in the home and then
> it progresses and the child goes to school, he
> is ill-prepared, he is in most cases not really
> ready, he finds himself becoming more and more
> backward, as a result he is ill at ease, he
> loses his confidence and self-respect with it
> and he is already on the way to feeling that he
> is a moron, and everything that he does and all
> the people around about him fairly rub this point
> of view in, so you are half-way to becoming a

delinquent. These are the kind of people generally who don't do well in school and who want to get the hell out of it as quickly as possible. These are the people who find themselves truanting and very often they become delinquent; the scene is set for it. If they don't become delinquent it's just as big an accident as it is to become a delinquent at that stage.

Other senior and social work staff also emphasise the part school plays in creating delinquency, although this is not emphasised so much as the family background. Dalmore social workers attempt to maintain contact with the home motivated by the knowledge that most boys will have to go home eventually, but they often feel that the most constructive way of dealing with the child's difficulties at school is to keep him at Dalmore until he has reached school leaving age. The feeling that 'very few are able to go back to school and make it' is typical. When the school leaving age was raised in 1973, however, it became apparent that many boys couldn't wait an extra year in Dalmore and would have to go back to school. Consequently the teaching programme was reorganised from its previous holding operation to a more subject-oriented programme that would help boys fit back into normal secondary school.

Subcultural explanations: General theories of delinquency in terms of peer group pressure are relatively rarely articulated. This may seem surprising given the immense amount of material produced by criminologists in the last twenty years, but is not so surprising given that there is very little that approved school staff can do about the gang structure in major cities. Sheriffs can send gang leaders away, but once they are away the institutional staff can only deal with the individuals not the gang. Further, the structure of local authority social work is set up to deal with families and individual casework, and neighbourhood community work is at present an experiment within an alien structure. Peer group pressures are often referred to by Dalmore staff, but not as a generalised philosophy; rather this is with reference to specific boys who either within Dalmore or while on leave are getting into further trouble. Subcultures come a poor third to family pathology and difficulties at school.

The key theme

The key link between Dalmore's view of the causes and the treatment of delinquency is the concept of the boy's 'problem'. It is assumed that boys get into trouble because they have 'problems'. This is illust-rated in the following answer by a social worker being questioned on his procedures when a new boy comes to the school:

> Well, first of all, we'd hope his local social worker has escorted him here. And if there's time I'll discuss with him the problems that he or she thinks have caused the breakdown....

That this is not the esoteric assumption of one man is demonstrated by the form which is routinely sent to all parents within a day of their boy arriving in the school. This form starts with the following instruct-ions:

> In order to help your son as much as we can, we would like to know more about him. It would enable us to understand his problems better if you would answer the following questions carefully.

Even before staff have met a boy, they assume that he has 'problems' and that he needs 'help' and 'under-standing'.

As with other aspects of the treatment model, the emphasis on each boy's 'problems' as the cause of his delinquency and the fit object for treatment is not peculiar to Dalmore. The White Paper, 'Children in Trouble' (HMSO 1968a: para.49) talks of children need-

28

ing 'to overcome their problems'; a discussion document by the Home Office Advisory Council (1970;67) emphasises the importance of 'a diagnosis of (the child's) problems'; Gill (1974) and Tutt (1974) report approved school staff frequently talking in the same terms, for example, 'the aim broadly speaking is to try to enable the kid to overcome his problems' (Tutt p.109); and Mason (1968) says that the aim of approved schools is 'that help may be given in an understanding of the underlying problems of the delinquent'. It is indeed now almost impossible to read discussion documents or articles about the aims of List D schools and community homes without finding the same terminology.

Boys' 'problems' as part of the Dalmore philosophy can be analysed into two closely related kinds. There are what could be called situational problems that reside in some situation outside Dalmore that the boy has had to cope with in the past and may have to cope with in the future, e.g. a step-father he does not get on with, a school he can't stand, local police who hound him, or unemployment. And there are personality problems which are more internalised, associated with the boy being labelled 'emotionally disturbed', these being seen as emanating from unsatisfactory homes. The two are closely related in that situational problems over time may create personality problems, and boys with personality problems may be less able than others to cope with situational problems.

Dalmore sees its task as helping with each boy's problems. This may mean changing his situation outside (although this is rarely possible), or it may mean enabling him to cope with the situation outside, or it may mean changing his internalised personality problem. Whichever of these is attempted though, Dalmore's attention is in some way focussed outside Dalmore - all boys' 'problems' either exist outside Dalmore (situational problems) or exist within the boy (personality problems) and have been caused by events outside Dalmore. There is never any hint of a view akin to that held by some about adult prisoners that their 'problems' are so internalised that they are now

unchangeable and that it is pointless to look outside
of the prison to the offender's background. The adolescent Dalmore boy is still too closely in touch with
his family and with other causal factors for all hope
of change to be dismissed. This commitment to the
boy's 'problems' which are located or originate outside
Dalmore is the core theme of the official philosophy,
a theme which is the continuing topic of enquiry
throughout this book.

2. *Individual treatment*

Boys' 'problems' are seen in Dalmore as the cause of
their delinquency and therefore as the object of
treatment. How does the school go about 'helping'
boys with their 'problems'? There are several parts
of the regime of the school which have been set up to
deal with this, and the crucial concept here is that
of 'individual treatment'. As each boy is seen as
being in the school not because he has committed an
offence but because he has a 'problem', this necess-
itates a regime that can cater for a variety of boys
each of whom has a different 'problem'. Associated
with this is the idea of 'shared responsibility' -
that boys must share in the process of treating each
other, and that the boys can be treated as rational
beings who can learn to look 'objectively' at their
own lives. Talk of 'individual treatment' and 'shared
responsibility' is increasingly common now in correctional institutions.

The basic aim of 'individually treating a boy's
problems' is recurrently given as the reason for
several aspects of the school. But the relationship
between philosophy and regime is not one of simple
causation - other institutions have much the same
official philosophy as Dalmore, but may have different
routines to implement it (compare Bottoms and
McClintock 1973:130-32). However, I want to show
briefly what the senior staff at Dalmore mean by
'individual treatment' by showing how they relate this
concept to three important aspects of the school's
regime:

i) The Boys' Hearings. A boy who misbehaves in Dalmore
may get referred to the Boys' Hearings which is a panel
of five boys and five staff. The headmaster describes
the aim of the Hearings to be 'individual treatment':

> ...A satisfactory conclusion doesn't mean that
> when a child has behaved badly and he is in
> serious trouble he gets the hammer for it, he
> loses all sorts of privileges and so on. A
> satisfactory conclusion is finding out why a
> thing happened, making sure that the child's
> personality is not attacked and destroyed in
> the process, trying to find out how we can
> possibly avoid a similar situation in the future,
> and at the end of the day helping the boy along
> the road towards release and towards living in
> the community.

ii) Group counselling. In group counselling the idea
is that each boy gains insight into his 'problems' and
into his environment through open discussion with
others having similar 'problems'. Important by-prod-
ucts of counselling are felt to be the education of
staff by the boys in the kind of background they come
from and the way they see life; and the reduction of
tensions within the school by the early verbal articulation of otherwise subversive elements within the
boys' subculture.

> Here we get the opportunity to look at the needs
> of the community, first of all as a community,
> then the smaller community of the houses, of
> the classrooms, of small groups in different
> settings, of the individual. In this way we
> can't lose sight of the individual because he
> has a voice there; if somebody can't use his
> own voice he always has a friend that will use
> his for him.

iii) Increase in frequency of leaves. During the research, home leave increased from once a month to once
a fortnight and then, for most boys, once a week. A
few years prior, leave had been only three times a

year. This change reflects the emphasis on the role
of the family and home community in the causation of
delinquency. This emphasis could be used to argue
that boys should be kept apart from their families
(Miller 1968:76), but Dalmore is in line with the more
common trend to maximise home leave. Facilitating
contact between boy, Dalmore and home is seen as a
positive step to resolving 'problems' to do with the
family. Also, a boy's behaviour on leave is seen as
a more reliable indicator of progress than his behaviour within Dalmore. Further, home leave is seen as
reducing the institutionalisation which is felt to be
so detrimental to the work of individual treatment and
shared responsibility.

THE VIEWS OF THOSE WHO DO NOT ARTICULATE THE OFFICIAL
PHILOSOPHY

One of the key aspects of group counselling in the
headmaster's view is that laymen rather than professional therapists are the counsellors so that counselling becomes an integral aspect of an institution,
rather than a professionalised speciality within it.
It is out of such groups, listening to children talking, that the headmaster claims his child-centred,
problem-oriented philosophy largely derives:

> I have learned far more from the children in
> group situations over the last ten to twelve
> years than I have learned all the time before
> that.

When the headmaster arrived at Dalmore he introduced
several of these ideas. Both those staff who articulate the official philosophy and those who have
reservations refer with deep feeling to the time
before the arrival of the present headmaster (a few
years before my research began). This period of the
school's history is rarely referred to in a disinter-
ested manner - rather it functions as a myth which
staff now use to legitimate their present beliefs.
The school at that time conformed more to the old

32

approved school model and training rather than treatment, correction rather than therapy, were the goals.
There is a certain amount of feeling by many staff
that much of what was good in the old regime has now
been lost.

If it is difficult to outline the themes of the
official philosophy, it is far more difficult to outline another coherent set of views held alongside or
in opposition to it. It is not that there are x
number of people who hold the official philosophy and
y who do not. Rather, there is a fairly coherent
official philosophy articulated by certain people in
certain situations, while other unofficial views find
expression in other situations. Although a few staunch
advocates of the official philosophy exist together
with a few staunch resisters of it, there are many more
staff who could not be categorised purely in terms of
their relation to the official philosophy. A model of
the staff as composed totally of 'goodies' and
'baddies', although implied by some staff themselves,
is not a model I wish to propose here.

Further, it is not that the senior staff hold a
coherent set of views, while the views of other staff
are fragmented, muted and incoherent. This is far
from the case and one could emphasise the inconsisten-
cies in the official philosophy and the simple traditional logic of some of the other views. However, the
situations in which senior staff find themselves, such
as sitting talking around the Board Room table and
talking to visitors, tend to aid the formulation of a
philosophy; while other staff only see each other at
coffee breaks and are not encouraged to air their
views to visitors and so their views become more fragmented. Thus, although the views of senior staff may
not, technically, be a philosophy, they are becoming
a philosophy; although not completely consistent or
shared in common they are becoming more consistent and
shared; whereas contrary views are becoming less of a
philosophy, and becoming more fragmented.

The variety of views held by staff is related to

33

their particular role in the school. On the whole,
professionally qualified social workers whose job is
largely to maintain contact with the family stress the
home as the major source of the children's troubles;
teachers who have left secondary schooling for the more
child-centred and remedial work of a List D school see
the importance of schooling and may emphasise the in-
adequacies of the children's previous schooling; trade
instructors stress the importance of good work habits
for the boy's future employment and future role as a
father; domestic staff mention the importance of good
food and clothing for the more materially deprived
children; and female staff often emphasise poor mother/
child relations and stress the role women can play in
the school.

A more important differentiation by role is that between those who are not continuously with boys (the
headmaster and social workers), and those who are and
are therefore in charge of them such that whatever job
they are officially doing they also have the task of
maintaining control. Given this distinction, it is no
surprise that criticisms of the official philosophy are
most often voiced in terms to do with the disciplinary
system of the school, a situation found in many correctional institutions (Conrad 1965; Polsky 1962).

What though are the views of the less powerful staff
about delinquency and their work with delinquents?
They are less interested in digging into a boy's past
in order to discover why he got into trouble unless the
boy himself raises it. Friendship with a boy is to
emerge on the basis of the interaction between the boy
and the staff member, not on the basis of the labels
attached to his file. As one part-time cleaner said:

> Ken, I just treat boys as I find them and if I
> do that they're fine. I dinna' ken what they're
> in for. Maybe if I did find out what they're in
> for, I wouldna see them quite the same way.

The part-time cleaner, like all staff, has access to
files. This is indeed fairly remarkable and there

cannot be many organisations where this is so. However it is social work staff who most regularly consult and create files for it is they who regularly correspond with other agencies and it is only they who have time specifically allocated for reading and writing letters and reports. Reticence to consult files is strongly associated with the lower status positions which are in turn strongly correlated with non-articulation of the official philosophy. Reticence to consult files does not necessarily mean, however, a commitment to regimentation and against 'individual treatment'. Low status staff may talk of becoming substitute mothers or fathers to specific boys in a very individualised way – the more one approximates a natural parent, I suppose, the less likely one is to consult or construct an extended written dossier on one's 'adopted child' and the more likely one is to 'just treat boys as I find them'. The philosophy of each boy having a 'problem' with which it is the school's task to 'help' implies that the 'problem' should be known about and written down, for every boy. The lack of commitment of many non-social work and non-teaching staff to discover a boy's recorded 'problems' indicates reservations about at least this aspect of the philosophy.

Although many staff are more concerned with meeting a boy as he is than with the 'causes' of delinquency, nevertheless all staff show some commitment to the rhetoric of 'it all starts in the home'. This is true with all, including those who are the severest critics of the official philosophy. For example, one man, who at the time of interview was notorious in senior circles for being against the philosophy in his handling of boys and who during interview showed considerable misunderstanding of the official philosophy, maintained:

> .....but, you know, ninety-nine per cent of those
> boys have got parents who have been cohabiting
> or divorced or are just not there at all.

To advocates of a 'training model', the theory that delinquents come from bad homes may often be associated

35

with the theory that there has been a lack of discipline at home so that the boys have not learned
society's values. It is then inferred that the
approved school should provide a tough but consistent
discipline.

Some staff, though, lack a general theory of delinquency and see a bad home not as an assumption on which
work with the children is based, but as an explanatory
device for the more exceptionally difficult, bizarre
or pathetic behaviour of a few boys. The rather spec-
ulative, impromptu reasoning employed here by one part-
time member of staff (who doesn't consult files)
illustrates this:

> Of course, you can tell a boy from a dirty home
> usually. It's just some sense of hopelessness
> about him. It's difficult to say. Sandy, for
> example. Someone was talking about him last week.
> He's a talented boy, he's a very nice boy, but I
> get the feeling he couldn't quite make it with
> himself somehow. And when someone told me that
> his home was very bad, that clicked with me.
> Also, I read in Spock, you know, the child-
> rearing man, that it's not good to allow small
> children to baby-sit a lot...I asked him what it
> was like in his home, and he said that he did do
> a lot of baby-sitting, and that all seemed to
> fit together for me. I mean, I sometimes wonder
> with these boys with only one parent, and there's
> men coming in and out of the house, I often wonder
> what it's like for them.

To conclude: The views of those who do not articulate
the official philosophy are diverse and increasingly
fragmented as they have lost any base of strength from
which to forward counter views. Their relative powerlessness described in the previous chapter has led to
their views having less influence over decisions on
boys' leave and release, and this is related to their
loss of influence in the ideological struggle. Thus,
although I have sketched some of their views and feelings, I do not propose to go into them in any more

36

.detail.

NOTES

(1)   In the terms of Street, Vinter and Perrow (1966: 49-63) this represents a shift from re-education/ development institutions to treatment institutions.

3   The boys' concerns

However, this bottle was <u>not</u> marked 'poison',
so Alice ventured to taste it, and found it
very nice (it had, in fact, a sort of mixed
flavour of cherry tart, custard, pine apple,
roast turkey, toffy, and hot buttered toast).
(Lewis Carroll)

In the previous chapter I examined Dalmore's official
philosophy - the view that the boys have 'problems'
that lie at the root of their getting into trouble.
In this chapter I shall introduce what I see as the
main concerns of the boys as seen by themselves, in
order to compare this with the official view. Do the
concerns that boys have relate to the 'problems' the
senior staff talk of? The official view states that
it is a resolution of these problems rather than mere
good behaviour that is required for a boy to be seen as
progressing and ready for release. What, though, do
the boys themselves think staff expect of them, do the
boys see good behaviour or the resolution of problems
as the way to get released?

GETTING OUT

Oh, I don't wanna' join the Dalmore life.
Gee boy, I wanna' go,
(Name of social worker) won't let me go,
Gee boy, I wanna' go home.

So runs the chorus to an old song, adopted by Dalmore
boys. Conditions in the school cannot be compared to
those in which slaves sang spirituals and press-ganged
men sang shanties expressing the same sentiment, or
even to the armed forces where this song possibly
originated, yet the boys' major concern is common to
all who have been compulsorily removed from home. TB

patients, mental patients, drafted soldiers, prisoners - all are denied 'the right to quit' and structure their lives in terms of that primary desire, 'I want to get out' (Roth 1963; 1973). As one Dalmore boy put it:

> Ken, you're wanting to see your mother, or your brothers an' that...you're wondering what they're doin' and what they're thinkin'.

As a corollary to getting out as the foremost concern is the view that although Dalmore is a 'cushy' place its main effect is that of punishment and deterrence (Gill 1974:108). The feeling of imprisonment over-rides any other idea as to what Dalmore is all about, and in this respect approved school is like many other institutions such as mental hospitals which inmates often experience as punishment. The view

> If I've got to be sent away I'd rather it was Dalmore than anywhere else but of course I'd rather be at home,

is the common response to the query, 'What do you feel about this place?' Indeed, Dalmore's cushiness heightens the anticipated deterrent effect in that the next List D school will not only remove you from home but will be worse than Dalmore. But it is the removal from home which is the really bitter pill. This is strikingly similar to Dunlop and McCabe's (1965) study of detention centres in which they conclude that although the regime is intended to be the opposite to Dalmore's - a 'short, sharp shock' that will act as a deterrent - yet it is still the loss of liberty that is the major experience of the men. Thus, whether the regime is severe as in detention centres or cushy as in Dalmore, it is the simple fact of being sent away that the boys are most concerned with.

Frequent leave, however, mitigates this:

> It's strange how folk talk of 'being inside'. Ken, you're only in a month and then every fortnight you're away and then if you stay on

you're away every weekend. You spend most of
the time outside!

Some boys put more value on leaves than do others. Just
as Irwin (1970:ch.3) has indicated that while physically in prison there are those who live their life
inside ('jailing') and those who live it outside
('doing time'), so there are differences in Dalmore
depending on previous biography and commitments and
the strength and frequency of contacts with significant
others outside. But even if a boy does discount his
time inside and lives for weekends, in so doing he
becomes very concerned about getting out - both every
week and for good. The more he lives for the weekend
the more 'getting out' becomes his major concern, and
the more the loss of freedom is felt during the week.

A few boys, however, ask to get sent away. One boy
said to me:

It was my idea to go intae an approved school.
I wanted approved school to keep me out of
trouble.

Typically, statements like this are met with surprise,
both by staff and by other boys. An explanation often
given by other boys is that 'he's got a spot of bother
at home'; the use of such an explanation for what is
seen as a strange and unusual desire indicates that the
boys generally expect each other to have homes that are
at least tolerable enough to go back to. This contrasts
with the official philosophy which sees family pathology as the rule rather than the exception. Strictly
speaking, although all boys want to get out, not quite
all want to go home. 'Going home' is often used
though as a generic term to mean 'going back to where
I came from' - and this may to the boys mean a foster
home, an uncle's, or an existence in the streets more
than in the house.

Most reasons given by boys who don't want to go on
leave concern what they see as only temporarily
abnormal situations at home or in the community:

40

When I was on leave I was being threated to
steal and my mother, father and sister were
being made a fool of and the boys have send
taxis to our door and they write on the door
and walls ect. I had my leave stopped but I
did not mind as I know what would happen, it
would be the same as the last time.
(diary)

This boy waited till the ring-leaders had been sent-
enced to Borstal and various other institutions and
then he felt it was safe to return. Life normally
back home was fine for him; it was just for the time
being that there were difficulties. Thus, those who
are not too keen on leave still want to get out for
good. One boy described what it was like on leave and
why:

If I lost a leave, maybe two, I wouldna' be
bothered. Him and her - my maw - she starts
arguin' wi' him. Aboot the Club...an' him...
an' she starts on me...an' then she starts on
my older brother 'cos he's in trouble again.
One thing leads tae anither an' then it's a
war an' I jist put on ma jaiket an' walk oot
o' the hoose.

Yet a couple of minutes earlier he had indicated that
being outside was preferable to being in Dalmore:

I'm no goin' to get in trouble again - I've
had enough o' bein' in here.

Boys for whom it eventually emerges there is no home
for them to go to, still want to get out - to digs, a
hostel, somewhere. Those few who don't want to get
home still want to get out.

'Getting out' can take four forms: for good (release),
regularly (leaves), whenever the opportunity arises
(outings), and running away (absconding). So far I
have restricted the discussion to release and leaves.
I will not consider absconding here because this is

41

not a concern that regularly affects all the boys.
There are times when a boy wants to run away, but apart
perhaps from the first day or two, running away is not
regularly considered as a means of getting out. Seiz-
ing opportunities during the week for getting out of
the grounds for a few hours or even minutes, however,
is a regular concern. There is a high rate of vol-
unteering for jobs outside the school, primarily
forestry and for a few weeks in summer grouse-beating,
even though this may be much more strenuous than work
inside. Trips to a local college for drama classes or
down the road to buy the day's papers are popular. The
main exceptions to the rule of maximising trips outside
the school are trips to the Sheriff Court or Children's
Hearings and to the dentist, although even here the
misery may be partially offset by the chance to get
into one's own clothes for a change.

One boy describes how physical removal from the
grounds is not enough. All semblance of inmate status
must be dispensed with:

> Mr V. said he would take ten boys to the wee
> shop down town so I was with the first lot, so
> we got in the van and went down to the shop. He
> stopped at a shop and said will you go in and
> get the papers so I went in and said to the guy,
> 'Have you got the papers ready yet?' and he said,
> 'Yes, sonny, here you are' and I got a big red
> face and was really mad at the way he talked and
> looked at me. Well, after that I jumped in the
> van and went down to another shop and it was my
> turn to go in the shop and I did not know the
> shop was packed with people or I would not have
> gone in with these daft school gear.
> (diary)

The wearing of school clothes outside the school is in
fact officially banned in an effort to reduce stigma
and institutionalisation. Neighbours report that
Dalmore boys are a lot less noticeable now than
formerly, but some anxiety about recognition remains
with the boys.

If one cannot get off from the buildings, maybe at least one can get off work. An attraction of the forestry work is the possible extension of lunch-breaks into a rabbit hunting expedition or some other activity completely removed from work and the school. Or a boy may describe with triumph how he has succeeded in getting allocated the cleaning of the toilets and has there slept undisturbed for an hour or so. Generally, however, work is not strenuous and so the main aim is not to get off it but to get away from the less pleasant jobs and away from the less pleasant people. Some of the jobs in the workshops are indeed highly valued (compare Dunlop 1975).

How to get out

If getting out is their major concern, how do boys ensure they get out as often as possible and out for good as quickly as possible? What kind of a performance do they think staff expect of them? Overwhelmingly, boys feel they have to 'do what the staff tell you', 'keep your nose clean' and 'behave yourself'. As I asked one boy:

- How long did it take you to settle?

- About three month.

- Why did it take that long?

- I dunno...I wasnae behavin' mysel' up in the bedrooms...I wis cheeky to the teachers... fly smokes and I got caught two or three times ...things like 'at.

- So what changed it then?

- Just thinkin'....whit's the use of goin' on this way, I'll never get oot o' here. I just started sayin' to mysel', I'm gonna' start behavin'.

Boys feel that if you behave you get good reports, and good reports get you out:

You've got to have good reports to get released. Billy, he's got bad reports for stealing and absconding.

Reports, then, are believed to consist of information about behaviour.

Whereas one has to behave in order to get released, getting leave is seen more as a right which comes automatically unless one is behaving badly; whereas one has to behave well to get released, one has merely not to behave badly to get leave. (In large measure it is also true that boys have merely not to behave badly in order to get released. If this is not quite realised by them, it may be because as one only gets released once there is always the fear that merely not behaving badly won't be enough, whereas with leave one soon has plenty of personal evidence that this is enough).

To conclude, the official philosophy and the boys' views on getting out may be contrasted as follows:

Boys' view	*Official philosophy*
1. Getting home is my major concern.	1. Getting home is the major concern of a boy.
2. To get home I must behave, that after all is why I am in here.	2. For him to get home, we should have sorted out his problems.
3. I will not get into trouble again as I do not want to be sent away again.	3. If a boy does well on release we hope it is because the treatment here has helped him.

I never heard any boy express the comprehension of the official philosophy that Gill (1974:120) reports of one highly intelligent fourteen year old:

All you gotta do is think up some problems and tell the staff. Like problems about your family and all that. Then they sort them out for you and they think you're getting better.

44

Gill notes that this view is very much the exception rather than the rule; it may be more common with older prisoners (Parker 1970:6; Millham et al. 1975:92).

KEEPING OUT OF TROUBLE

> The new boys in our dorm have settled down
> except one is making too much noise. We have
> been getting in too much trouble as the office
> is directly beneath us and they could almost
> hear a pin drop.

Since behaviour is seen as the way to get out, behaviour becomes a major concern and this is true for all boys, even those whose behaviour staff see as disruptive. All boys see a need to behave. But they also have other concerns - such as not being seen to 'sook' (to curry favour with staff), getting on with the boys, maintaining comforts, having fun - and the fulfilment of these other concerns may lead to behaviour which gets them in trouble.

There are two ways in which boys are concerned about their behaviour, and these are described by Matza (1964:88) as the moods of humanism and of fatalism:

> The delinquent is subject to frequent oscillation
> between sensing himself as cause - humanism -
> and seeing himself as effect - fatalism.

When in the mood of fatalism we see our behaviour not as something that we ourselves have done but something that 'they' have arbitrarily defined that we have done, something not that we have done but that they have done to us. Bad behaviour is something that happens, not that we make happen. If it is felt to be arbitrary whether staff object to what one is or is not doing, then it becomes pointless considering the legitimacy of one's activities. Engaging in illicit activities is seen not as misbehaviour, but as gambling or risk-taking; in this mood the concern with behaviour is the concern with fate. The boy who says

45

'I'm no' bothering', 'I couldna' care', is saying that
he isn't bothering to try to control his behaviour
since this is as impossible as controlling his fate.
He is very concerned, though, about his behaviour,
about his fate.

In the mood of humanism the boy <u>decides</u> to behave.
The most frequently referred to means of achieving
this is to avoid bad company. It is mentioned in
Chapter 5 that the main explanation parents use regarding their child's being in trouble is that other boys
get him into trouble. This theory of trouble is thus
readily available to a List D boy from his past, so he
may decide that 'the pals I pal about with' in the
school are crucial. I asked one boy how easy it is to
keep out of trouble at Dalmore:

> Och, nae bother. You find oot a lot o' boys
> that's just deliberate trouble-makers an' you
> go an' find some boys that's peace-makers....
> likes o' Billy...you winna' catch him daein'
> nuthin' wrang...so I just says Billy's a good
> loon, he likes things that I like, showed him
> over the place an' he's turned oot good....so
> efter that I says, 'Well, that's a mate'...
> Me an' Billy...I'd be no' only loosin' a mate
> I'd be loosin' a partner, see, I couldna' say
> nuthin' against Billy and he couldna' say nuthin'
> against me.

Other boys feel that the safest policy is to isolate
yourself. This has the double advantage that it is
easier to behave well as there are no boys you are
committed to who will lead you into illicit activities,
and if you personally decide to behave badly there is
no-one else to 'grass' you. Isolation aids good behaviour and reduces the chances of getting caught for
bad behaviour. But isolation may have its costs, such
as low status. Also a boy may not choose to be an
isolate, he may be forced into it because of being
seen as of low status by others.

A boy's decision to behave well can often be seen by

other boys as sooking, and this can lead to a deter-
ioration of relations with them. Also a boy may see
reporting to staff on other boys' behaviour as a way
of behaving well; but this is likely to be seen by
other boys as grassing, which can also lead to deteriorating relations. Thus the concern to behave and the
concern to get on with the other boys can often conflict. This is especially so for boys already of low
status among their peers, for they are particularly
liable to being labelled a sook or a grass - the label
may often follow low status rather than produce it.

The concern with behaviour is linked to the view
that behaviour goes into reports, and reports affect
release. Staff encourage boys to take the humanistic
rather than the fatalistic view of behaviour. But the
official philosophy also claims that release and reports are based on all kinds of things as well as behaviour - factors such as maternal deprivation, sub-
cultures and housing which deterministic criminology
claims cause delinquency. As Matza says (1964:89-90),
determinism is a handy tool to uphold the mood of
fatalism in an era when supernatural bases for fatalism are becoming less available. Thus, even if the
boy believes as is told him that all kinds of things
affect his release, there is only one of these that he
can approach in a mood of humanism, that is, his behaviour, and even this he is not constrained to approach
in the mood of humanism, even this he can be fatalistic
about. This is shown in the following diary extract in
which the boy is going to a Review Hearing - he has
not been to a Children's Panel previously as he was
committed before April 1971 by a court - and he learns
to his surprise that more than his behaviour is to be
taken into account. But only his behaviour - including
his work - is under his control, and even his good
behaviour is something not that he does but that he is
told about. The only way he can control the other
relevant factors is by a purely negative removal from
them by not going on leave, and even this course of
action was something not that he did, but that Dalmore
did and he agreed to:

47

Today (housemaster) told me to come to his
office for he wanted to make my report for the
panel it was not quite what I expected as the
pannal look into everything. I was told that
I was well behaved and worked hard.

GETTING ON WITH THE OTHER BOYS

My housemaster came up to me and said would I go
down into town to do a job for him and I said,
'If you tell me who's going' and he said, 'Does
it matter' and I said 'Yes'. So he told me and
the people who were going suited me so I went.

Insofar as List D schools are seen from the outside as
the severest punishment that can be meted out to a boy
under fifteen, a boy expects to find there boys much
harder than he and this can prove to be anxiety-
provoking even for the toughest boy (Sykes 1965:77).
And even if he finds they are not that hard, he still
has the problem of surviving in a closed community - a
concern shared for example by public school-boys and
soldiers. Two anxieties especially are felt, anxieties which are often two sides of the same interactional
coin: fear of being bullied, and coping with boys who
provoke you.

Fear of being bullied

This fear varies depending on who is in the school.
Sometimes there is public recognition of a major bully
or gang; at other times life can be relatively quiet.
How may a potential victim protect himself? Isolation
is one possibility; as one boy who was often to be
found sitting on a remote window ledge buried deep in
his comic, said:

I just walk away fae them....just keep right out
their road. But ken they come lookin' for you
and when they see you they just shove you about.

If isolation doesn't work, more drastic measures may

have to be taken, such as running away. This solves
the immediate problem for the boy in that it removes
the thorn from his flesh but as he is running away
from something rather than to anywhere he may find himself caught between the Devil (his aggressor) and the
deep blue sea (130 miles of darkness on a winter's
night between Dalmore and home).

If isolation and running away are not successful,
then a boy may request official isolation in the
Cottage or legitimating his desire to run away by asking for a transfer to another List D school. In the
Cottage there is always a significant proportion of
smaller boys who would concur with the view of one
particularly frail and weepy boy:

> I didna' like the school. Too much bullyin'
> in the school. I was gettin' shoved about in
> the school.

Requests for a transfer to another school, however, are
very rarely granted. This is for at least two reasons,
one on the boy's part and the other on the staff's.
There is continuous propaganda that Dalmore is better
than any other List D school and most of the boys
believe this (1) and consequently requests for transfer
can easily be dampened by reminding the boy of how he'd
be worse off in other schools. On the staff side, they
want to minimise transfers as transfers imply failure
and involve asking a favour of another school which
diminishes Dalmore's balance in the bank of favours
between itself and other schools. One alternative is
to release the bully (chapter 6). Once when this
solution was achieved, another boy reported to me with
some feeling:

> He didna' get aff my back. When he got released
> ....just....heaven came doon!

Bullying is a concern of those who feel they are
bullied, and a concern of the staff. The boy who is
labelled as a bully never accepts the label; a boy may
admit to grassing or sooking, but never to bullying.
The concerns of the boy so labelled are maybe to do

having fun, as described later in the chapter, or possibly he is concerned about 'being provoked', a concern
shared by many others.

Being provoked

Sometimes the boy others label a bully says in defence,
'I had to hit him, he was provoking me, getting on my
wick'. One biggish boy in the Cottage describes this
experience:

> For the first couple o' month I was doin' brilliant
> and then I started getting fouled up by all they
> bams likes of wee (names three small boys). Ken,
> all the wee boys that get on your wick. They
> come up to me and say 'You got your hand on me!'
> - ken they get on your wick, they talk aboot ye
> and they'll come up and try and sook up, ken
> when you're trying to do your job in the morning.
> They'll muck you up, and ken you lose your heid
> wi' some o' them. And you feel in a bad mood
> all morning. You kick somebody and you get a
> bad report.

This kind of situation is frequent in a school where
although the age range is apparently narrow, i.e.
thirteen to fifteen, there is all the difference between a small thirteen-year old and a large fifteen-year
old. Small boys resent 'the big boys who think they're
hard men' and big boys resent 'they wee bams'.

Provocation may not just come from boys who are too
small for one to safely hit in return. All kinds of
apparently trivial things may annoy one:

> Today I was playing fivestones which is a popular
> game in school just now and this boy wouldn't
> stop pestering me and saying things about my mate
> who brings me sweets every day and he is jealouse
> and make a fool of us as he calles us names and
> he all ways follows us around and even spies on us.
> (diary)

50

Being called names can be especially aggravating. The violent response this produced in a boy who had had the misfortune to have an operation on his testicles is described by one of his few friends.

> I thought he was a good lad. In a way he was a
> bully. In another way, ken, if you got on wi'
> him a' right - but naebody wanted to get on wi'
> him - I liked him. I got on wi'him a'right. He
> used tae stand up for me when I first came in.
> But naebody wanted tae like him. They liked
> takin' the mick oot o' him, 'cos they kennt he'd
> go daft. Lose his temper - like if ye ca'd him
> 'Oddball' an' that. If people ca' ye names, that
> can make you crack up. And naebody's wanting tae
> like ye, ken.

The difficulties caused by the concern to get on with other boys, like the concern with status, complicates the business of behaving well.

COMFORT

> It's dead cushy - just like Butlins.

In any institution where one has to live twenty-four hours a day and where, on the whole, facilities are provided for you rather than by you, the maintenance of certain comforts becomes a major concern. The most obvious of these in Dalmore is smoking for, although smoking is allowed, the amount allowed is considerably less than some boys are accustomed to. The first impression of a visitor to an approved school is often that of virtually every boy asking you if you can spare a cigarette; although such requests are more tempered in Dalmore, the visitor or newcomer soon becomes aware that 'smokes' is still a problem for many boys.

The official smoking times are for some the focal points around which the day is timetabled, punctuated by bonuses of extra smokes. One boy's description in his diary of a total day was:

51

> Got up, got breakfast 5 to 8 went in the kitchen
> till parade then on parade. fell out and went to
> my daily job in the laundry, break came and got
> a smoke from McIntosh. went to work again and
> swept the dorms, and fixed the beds got dinner
> then got another smoke from mcintosh went to work
> finish 5 past 3 had a game of football then got
> tea. At night I polish the classroom A. then
> talked to the woman student for some time then
> got sprayed, night bun and smoke and up and watched
> the Avenjers watched tv all time tell lights out
> then bed.

Possibly the smokes he got from McIntosh were additional ones out of official smoking times, possibly he had
run out due to bad management as it was near the end of
the week and he had to cadge off the other boy. Either
way the smokes from McIntosh were minor triumphs notable for the day's diary.

Tobacco (or sweets for non-smokers) has to last the
whole week and good management is required. One
illicit method of management is described:

> Me and (another boy) didna' give in the money
> we brought back from leave last weekend and we
> kept it upstairs, and every day when the message
> boy goes down to the shop for the paper he gets
> us some sweeties.

Tactics for hoarding cigarettes and matches are more
dangerous than for sweets as it is not illegal to have
sweets on the person, whereas it is to have cigarettes
and matches. A boy was talking with me about his trade
instructor:

> He's a rat. See, if he sees you bangin' a match?
> He says, 'Where did you get that match?' an' he
> goes intae everythin' aboot where you got it an'
> 'Where you come by that' an' all that.

Other staff are less inquisitorial and may merely con-
fiscate or even ignore it. But you can't tell who's

going to catch you and so the whole operation is risky.

One method of managing scarce resources such as smokes is the 'halfer' system in which a boy selects a pal with whom he commits himself to go halves on any valuable commodity that comes his way. The prevalence of this system is waning as tobacco is now more readily available due to the legalisation of smoking and the increased number of leaves. Informal agreements still arise over the sharing of other valued goods, such as transistor radios, but there is no longer the need for a stable halfer as there was when tobacco was illicit and home leave much rarer. But even then the halfers system was not perfect as it could easily lead to exploitation:

> Well, halfers was a no' bad idea. You know you found a really good mate, but that was the worst thing - you didna' ken who was good or no. 'Cos as soon as you walked in the door (as a new boy) everyone's saying, 'You be my halfer?' Some daft boy says, 'Aye, I'll be your halfer' and the guy takes all your smokes off you and doesna' give you nought. Best to take halfers wi' someone who's a really good mate.

Some comforts are scarce, but to concentrate on scarcity would be misleading for Dalmore is commonly seen as 'cushy'. But this often implies it should be 'stricter', as one boy complained to me:

> The boys get aff wi' blue murder. Like swearin' at the teachers an' everythin.
> Some of the teachers say something to them or 'I'll tell the Guv' (headmaster) and others just dinna bother.

> See this gettin the smoking room an everythin' all decorated, that'll no make much difference. That's just goin to make everybody act the goat there, isn't it? Smokin' room, swimmin' pool, aye an ken the back door as you're going in? Well, (the painting instructor) put a new glass windae

there aboot a month ago. An' it wis just
smashed.

There is a contradiction in the way the lack of strictness is described (compare Millham et al. 1975:108).
On the one hand, the school is criticised for its lack
of strictness and this is given to account for why so
many boys get into trouble again, but when the lack of
strictness is related to the boy himself, his attitude
changes. Firstly, he's not going to get into trouble
as, although Dalmore is cushy, the next place won't be.
Secondly, those instances of strictness he has experienced he may not approve of. Although many would
agree with one boy's view that,

> the parades (roll-calls) are too cushie. If
> they were more strict I think most boys would be
> more disciplined,

others have criticised the few staff who run parades
strictly, and one temporary member of staff who had
been seconded from the Army was informally criticised
for 'thinking he's still in the army'.

What then do boys mean by 'cushiness' if it is both
criticised and enjoyed? The simultaneous enjoyment
and criticism of cushiness can only be understood if
cushiness is seen as 'lack of strictness', i.e. if
cushiness is defined on a dimension of punitiveness.
That is, boys see Dalmore as low in punitiveness. In
these terms, the school is 'not strict enough' on the
reasoning that - 'List D schools are punitive establishments, and if you ask me to judge this school I can
only do so in those terms and judge it as not strict
enough'. On the other hand cushiness is enjoyed on the
reasoning - 'Of course, I'm glad the school is cushy,
as it makes life easier'.

This view of cushiness contrasts with the headmaster's who sees it as the outworking of a therapeutic
regime leading to relaxed and informal relations -

> I know they call this place 'Butlins' and

54

'Dalmore Hotel'. They know it's easier here,
but that's because the relations here are better.

Were boys to explain cushiness in similar terms they
would approve of as well as enjoy the cushy regime.

HAVING FUN

Having fun is a major concern which the boys import
with them when they come into Dalmore. One of Walter
Miller's (1958) focal concerns of lower class culture
is 'excitement'; a similar term used about and possibly
by British working class adolescents a few years ago
concerning some of their more newsworthy performances
was that they were doing it 'for kicks'. Albert Cohen
(1965) has stressed the delinquent's emphasis on short-
run hedonism, Becker (1963) says marihuana smoking
should not be seen as serious activity but as fun, and
a recent set of interviews with some Scottish approved
school boys listed 'fun' as their most frequent
'perceived reason for delinquency' (McMichael 1972).
Armstrong and Wilson (1973:67) and Words from an East
End Gang (1972) vividly document fun as characterising
the life-style of British adolescent gangs; Parker
(1974:67) considers that monetary reward did not
replace fun as the motive for thieving among his
Liverpool boys until their mid-teens. What adults call
'delinquency' is for many boys a very minor and episodic part of the more important business of having fun
(Matza 1964).

Blumenstiel (1973) goes further. Doing things just
for fun, just to have a good time, is by no means only
a concern of deviants but is a characteristic way in
which members of our society account for good times.
Aries' (1973) implies that having fun has not always
been seen as the legitimate activity or preserve of
children. Possibly it is only in this century that
having fun, playing, is something not only that children may do but that is seen as positively educational
for them. In more hedonistic cultures it is maintained
that fun is good not only for children but for all; in

puritanical cultures having fun may be seen as evil. Given such variation from one culture to another it is also reasonable to expect that within any one culture what one person may define as fun, another may not.

A wide range of activities is described by boys at Dalmore as fun. My impression is that Dalmore boys account for their behaviour as fun no more nor less than, say, my personal friends or academic colleagues, but that such accounts are often more noticeable as the actions referred to are not seen as fun by other people such as policemen, householders or List D staff and so these people may try to stop or spoil the boys' fun. Consequently, having fun can become problematic for Dalmore boys. Having fun legitimately is not always easy for them, and so becomes a major concern.

I will now examine some of the ways in which other people in Dalmore define activities which a boy defines as fun.

One way in which staff define boys who are having fun is to describe them as 'high'. This corresponds to an aspect of the boy's experience, namely that they feel they have some power over and can transcend the material world. This experience is related to being high on alcohol or LSD. For example, after one's football team has just beaten its chief rivals one may (accurately) feel one has the power to walk down the middle of the town's main street without being subject to the normal physical probability of being run down by a car or stopped by the police. This particular experience is only possible when in company, but being 'high' may also describe more individual behaviour in which normal physical laws are not experienced as operating; or in which the person feels that he can transcend social laws and is free to do things he may not normally do. This is akin to Matza's (1964:69) idea of drift as 'episodic release from moral constraint'.

When staff see a boy as high, their first aim is to bring him 'down', which if the boy has been having fun in company, may simply mean isolating him. In an

56

institution like Dalmore, news can travel fast and this
may provide staff with enough information for them to
guess why a boy is high and so they may impute dimin-
ished responsibility and neutralise what might otherwise be seen as an offence.

Being high, though, often involves treading on other
people's feet. There are often others around who are
not having fun or are not high and who consequently
experience the fun-makers' freedom as impinging on
their own freedom. Fun-making is often accompanied by
fun-spoiling. Boys in List D schools have had a long
experience of police, teachers, parents, neighbours
etc. 'spoiling our fun'. (The coup de grace of this
process is to be sent away, for this not only spoils
whatever fun was being had before but, it is anticipated, ensures that not much more fun can be had for
quite a while). If the person at whose expense the fun
has been had is a smaller boy, then allegations of
bullying may be made in which the smaller boy and
adults may form a coalition in opposing the definition
of fun. For example, a boy is at the Boys' Hearings
for absconding:

Boy One:	Me and (Boy Two) play with him but he doesn't take it as fun.
Staff One:	If he doesn't take it as fun, then it isn't fun.
Boy One:	But he can't take fun.
Staff Two:	But when you're playing with a boy and he starts crying then it becomes bullying.
Staff Three:	I think (Boy Two) means it in fun, but he's a big boy and he doesn't know when to stop.

There are situations, though, which one boy defines
as fun but others don't but which the others come to
accept as fun. If the fun-maker can persuade the
others that it's fun after all he may earn the label
of a 'comic' or a 'good laugh'.

A boy may, however, go far further than anyone else

57

would dream of in defining a situation as fun, and this may earn him the label of being 'mental'. This term contains a strange mixture of admiration and connotations of mental illness derived from the unpredictability of the behaviour. The art of judging exactly how far one may go in having fun is a fine one, and the successful fun-maker is liked by all, boys and staff. To be too successful with staff, though, may lead to allegations of sooking.

To switch to the opposite extreme, accounting for some behaviour as fun may incur the staff's displeasure. Although staff often among themselves use 'fun' as an explanation for many boys' misdemeanours and neutralise the misdemeanours with comments such as 'boys will be boys' or 'I did the same at his age', nevertheless once a boy has formally been defined as having committed an offence, woe betide him or other boys who try to describe the offence to staff as fun. Any school-boy knows the likely effect on the teacher of giggling while an offender is being interrogated. To define the offence or the interrogation as fun is to deny not that the boy is responsible for the offence but to deny that the offence was an offence and to challenge the authority of the teacher to define what is and is not trouble. The most explosive reactions by staff that I observed were produced by such acts of defiance; for example, a new boy was returned after having absconded:

Headmaster:	What happened when you went?
Boy:	It was fun. I'd do it again.
Headmaster:	(torrential response lasting several minutes including such statements as)
	— I'll not have a boy speak like that!...I won't have it!...I can have you locked up right away, make no mistake!...I've been in this work twenty years and I've never heard an attitude like that!...I've not used the belt since I've been here but I feel so angry just now I feel like really knocking some sense into you!

58

(requests a member of staff to fetch
the two belts from their ceremonial
glass cupboard.)
Choose which one you'd like. I'll
show you what it'd feel like on your
backside!
(lashes the table with the belt. The
boy, expressionless up to now, starts
sobbing.)
Well, have you got anything to say?

Before staff can convert a boy to the philosophy that
he is in the school because of personal 'problems'
rather than because of 'bad behaviour' it must be
agreed that there is something 'wrong' with the boy or
his situation in the first place. This is totally
undermined if the boy denies anything is wrong by saying, 'It was fun'.

Having fun in Dalmore, then, may often create difficulties for boys and, insofar as they are aware of
this, having fun constitutes a concern of theirs. 'Fun'
is an important concept if we are to understand a boy's
definitions of a whole range of activities that others
may variously define as 'insolence', 'cheek', 'bullying', 'stupidity', 'sooking' or 'inexplicable'. A boy
concerned both to have fun and to behave well may find
these incompatible.

The boys' view of fun may be contrasted with the
official philosophy in various ways. Insofar as activity that staff see as trouble is seen as fun by the
boys, boys do not see a need for an explanation or
account of such activity. Staff informed by a philosophy which seeks underlying causes to deviant behaviour
and boys who see such behaviour as fun and hence normal
may have communication difficulties. Further, to be
asked to analyse how you've been having fun is less fun
than the experience of actually having the fun, and the
official philosophy encourages boys to analyse why they
get into trouble. Descriptions boys give to their pals
about past offending often refer to fun, and the act of
describing is often fun too. But rarely is it fun to

59

offer an account for, say, the Boys' Hearing; and if
fun is offered as an account there this leads to displeasure from staff.

RESUME AND PREVIEW

The major concerns that I have so far depicted affect
all boys in Dalmore at least some of the time. They
obviously do not exhaust the concerns that boys have,
but these five - getting out, keeping out of trouble,
having fun, getting on with the other boys, and
comfort - encompass all the major concerns that are
felt by all of the boys. These daily concerns do not
coincide with the problems that the official philosophy claims need solving; it is not so much that they
are in head-on collision, but that often they simply
do not meet. This has been documented in other studies. Bottoms and McClintock (1973:228), for example,
found in their Borstal that 'the inmates were a good
deal more optimistic about future social problems than
were the staff'. Quite marked differences were recorded; for example, whereas Borstal staff thought
eighty per cent of boys 'required attention' over
family problems, only eight per cent of boys 'anticipated considerable problems' and sixty per cent were
'very confident - no problems foreseen' (pp.192-226).
A study in a Californian prison shows the same sort of
divergence between the counsellor who sees psychological therapy as important and the prisoner who considers his problems to reside in the nature of the
prison itself (Manocchio and Dunn 1970:20). That the
concerns of staff and inmates at Dalmore diverge is
common to other correctional institutions. This divergence is important for those who attempt to run therapeutic regimes in such institutions for it is unlikely
that therapy will succeed if the two parties define the
situation in diverging ways (Dunlop 1975; Gill 1974:
17-18).

At Dalmore, the senior staff see their work as identifying and treating the 'problems' they see associated
with the boys being in trouble. The boys, however, see

60

as quite normal those aspects of their lives that
others define as delinquency. Crime is a minor part of
a lifestyle which is taken for granted and unproblematic, or unproblematic at least until they get sent
away (Jones 1968:67). There is little reason why they
should seek to understand or explain their delinquency.
They may well experience problems in the family or
elsewhere but there is little reason why they should
relate these to their being in trouble and to the task
of getting out of Dalmore. Rather, while in Dalmore,
they are concerned about, in addition to getting out,
such things as behaving well, getting on with the other
boys, keeping comfortable and having fun. It is not
that they necessarily deny that they have problems at
home, but that such problems are deemed irrelevant by
them to the business of getting out of Dalmore. Whereas
in staff's eyes the boys' problems preceded their committal to Dalmore, indeed caused their committal, in
boys' eyes their concerns all derive from having been
sent away, indeed are caused by their committal.

I am not arguing that staff are unaware of the boys'
concerns. They are very aware, and indeed have re-
structured the school regime very much in order to
meet exactly the concerns I have described in this
chapter. But in the view of the official philosophy,
meeting these concerns is only a means towards the
'real' work of the school which is the individualised
treatment of emotional and other personal problems
originating outside Dalmore. This divergence between
the boys' concerns and the problems that the senior
staff believe that they have raises at least three
questions, and Part Two will try to answer these.

Firstly, how is it that two such divergent foci of
attention can co-exist? How can staff and boys having
concerns that do not really meet co-exist in an institution that involves a high degree of contact between
staff and boys all day and every day? How does each
of the two views resist erosion by the other?

Secondly, each side - boys and senior staff - have a
model of what Dalmore is all about: as either a

61

therapeutic establishment for the resolution of personal problems, or as a punitive institution to be got out of as soon as possible by means of behaving well. Is one of these two models in fact more accurate than the other? For example, are boys released from Dalmore on the basis of resolution of their personal problems or as a result of good behaviour within Dalmore?

Thirdly, are the therapeutic goals of the senior staff successfully implemented? If not, does the different definition of the school that the boys hold help account for the failure of therapy? Is it in fact possible for staff to diagnose, let alone solve, the problems that they assume boys have? Most studies evaluating correctional institutions proceed by comparing reconviction rates from various kinds of traditional and experimental regimes; this may (often it does not though - see Clarke and Cornish 1972) tell us what kind of regime is the most successful, but because there is little analysis of the processes operating within each regime there are few clues available as to why any one regime is more or less successful.

It has been suggested by some who know Dalmore, and more closely argued by observers of other schools (e.g. Gill 1974:46-7; Polsky 1962), that if the official philosophy is not fully implemented this is because lower level staff hold more traditional views (Chapter 2) and are preoccupied with the daily tasks of feeding, clothing, amusing and controlling the inmates so that the goal of 'treatment' goes by default. Also, as it is these middle and junior level staff that the boys are in hour-by-hour contact with, this explains why the boys do not see the school in terms of the official philosophy. To some extent this is true of Dalmore, but were this the whole story, my story would end here. Yet another sad case of the expressive goals of senior staff displaced by the organisational goals of other staff, of a progressive headmaster thwarted by the traditionalism of his staff. The end.

But this is by no means the whole story. It is the senior staff who have power to grant release and home leave, to meet these major concerns of each boy. Thus, senior staff are crucial to the implementing of the philosophy, and however much the views of other staff rub off onto the boys through regular contact nevertheless the boys know that it is senior staff who control release and leaves, and consequently boys are concerned to discover the criteria senior staff use in arriving at release and leave decisions. Practically, the senior staff's perspectives are more crucial for boys than are the views of other staff.

In attempting to understand the interface between the boys' and the staff's perspectives then, I propose in Part Two to look in detail at some of the work of senior staff. I will argue that they face constraints and difficulties inherent in operationalising a treatment philosophy. Thus, even if all the Dalmore staff were united in favour of the treatment model, and even if middle and lower level staff could devote themselves to the 'individual needs' of the boys rather than to the physical needs of the boys and of the buildings, even so there would be a divergence between staff and boys' perspectives and the treatment model would not be fully implemented.

The procedure I will use is to look at the information on boys routinely available to senior staff, at the procedures they use to convert this information into 'problems' that boys have, and at how this process is related to the official philosophy and to the boys' concerns.

NOTES

(1)   This preference for one's own school over others is typical in most approved schools (Dunlop 1975:24).

63

PART II

PROBLEM SOLVING

4   Talking about "problems"

> *'I'm sure those are not the right words', said*
> *poor Alice.*
> *(Lewis Carroll)*

The most readily available source of information about
a boy's 'problems' is the boy himself, but how productive is he of the information that senior staff want?
To answer this I will ask the following questions: how
does a boy view the giving of information about himself, his family and his situation outside Dalmore?
has he the language and models at hand to provide
information in the form staff want? in what kinds of
situations do staff attempt to elicit such information
from a boy? are there routine situations which provide
such information, or do staff have to rely on exceptional occurrences or crises which bring the boy to
talk about his 'problems'?

THE BOYS' ORIENTATION TOWARDS TALKING ABOUT 'PROBLEMS'

Boys are more concerned with getting out of trouble
than with analysing how they got into trouble. For
them, trouble means getting caught and getting sent to
a List D school. Their concern is to get out of the
List D school. Trouble as defined by Dalmore staff
and other agencies, namely offences committed or
'anti-social behaviour', is not something which boys
generally see as requiring explanation.

Boys often experience problems at home, at school
and in other situations outside, but they have not
become familiar with the model of delinquency that
relates such problems to their delinquency. Indeed,
they have not become familiar with the notion that
events in the years preceding their offending are
important (compare Macintyre 1977). Rather, they are

concerned with events in the months and years following
and consequent on their offending. They do not come to
Dalmore realising that presenting anxieties about home
and life outside may be something expected of them as
an integral part of being a good inmate. This is not
to say that they do not have anxieties, fears or
'problems'. Children with a recently acquired step-
parent, or a father in prison, or an alcoholic mother,
or experiencing intimidation or failure at school are
all very likely to have fears and anxieties about such
things and many Dalmore boys do indeed have such things
to cope with. But they do not immediately define such
fears and anxieties as relevant to the task of getting
out of Dalmore. Unless a boy is particularly worried
about some situation outside there is no special reason
why he should talk about, say, his family or his secondary school to staff in Dalmore.

Going home on leave every fortnight or every week
militates against boys learning the philosophy that
delinquency is caused by problems at home. On leave
they renew contact with parents and peers who have
ideas about delinquency that differ from the staff's
(Taylor 1971:24). Paradoxically, the treatment philosophy sows the seeds of its own destruction here; it
emphasises that boys should not become institution-
alised and should go home frequently to face up to
their problems, but in so doing limits the effective-
ness of the institution as a means of resocialising the
boys into accepting the philosophy.

Although boys do not believe that all boys in List D
schools have problems in the family or elsewhere that
preceded and caused their getting into trouble, they do
believe that a minority of other boys, other than oneself, has problems at home. There are regular refer-
ences made about other boys who talk about intimate
family matters in public situations, and such refer-
ences indicate that this is seen as inappropriate, or
sad, or pathetic:

> Duncan McQuade, he used to sit in the leave bus
> with me, and my ma would see me off and he'd be

all over her to come up to Dalmore. He'd say,
'My maw's fucking drunk, she got a bottle of wine
last night'...That's terrible that.

Very often a reputation of having family problems is
used by other boys to excuse behaviour which is seen as
'psyche' or 'nuts', i.e. to excuse an abnormal state
of affairs (Walter 1975b). The family pathology model
is here seen as appropriate not for normal delinquency
but for psychological abnormality, i.e. for a minority
of boys.

Allegations of family pathology are also used to rank
very low status boys; the labels 'bastard' and 'orphan'
are particularly potent weapons against a boy who is in
fact and knows himself to be a bastard or an orphan.

A few boys see themselves as 'in care', and these are
often those who have been committed to Dalmore not
following an offence but for care and protection. Such
boys emphasise that 'I'm not in here for stealing; it's
because I don't get on at home'. Thus, these boys who
do explicitly talk about themselves having family problems do not link this to delinquency since they do not
see themselves as delinquents. By claiming 'I'm not
like you lot - you're all thieves' such a boy can defend
his reputation against imputations of being 'psyche',
an 'orphan', or whatever. At the same time he implicitly rejects the treatment model philosophy that family
pathology leads to delinquency.

That boys generally only refer to other boys having
family problems indicates three basic assumptions held
by most boys at Dalmore: 1) it is inappropriate to talk
in public about things awry in one's own family; 2)
those that do talk in this manner are a minority; 3)
those that do have something wrong with them. These
assumptions are also revealed in certain objections to
some aspects of the Children's Hearings. As I recorded
one conversation:

John: I think the panel's a good thing.
           They find out all about you; that's

69

good, isn't it?

George: I dinna' think so. You dinna' like being asked whether your dad drinks or whether he hits your ma.

John: All right, they shouldna' ask questions like that.

Boys, then, do not usually see it as appropriate to talk about family or other kinds of problems indicated by the official philosophy, and even if they do they may find it difficult to find an appropriate occasion on which to make such problems public. There are also other things which may inhibit boys discussing what staff would define as pertinent problems. One is that what staff may define as pathological the boy may not, and another is that the leaking of certain information about family or other situations outside may incriminate the boy. Both of these are illustrated in the following conversation between two boys and myself. The conversation was a bragging session late one night in which one boy was recounting and probably embellishing one of his more ardent undetected exploits. He claimed to have stolen a large sum of money:

Researcher: What did you spend it on?

Jimmy: Record player, tape recorder, gave £60 to my ma.

Researcher: Where did your ma think you'd got this lot from?

Jimmy: Aw, she knows I've knocked it. But she wouldna' grass me.

Willie: Nor mine. I ken a boy who stole some money and his ma phoned the police. Fancy grassing your own son!

The conversation continued to affirm that being grassed by one's own parents is not acceptable. Jimmy's parents, were their failure to report their son known by staff, would be seen by staff as requiring some kind of social work intervention. There would be seen to be 'problems' in such a family. But Jimmy and Willie do not see such parents as pathological; indeed, they see

70

them as normal and morally in the right. So this is what staff would define as a 'problem' at home but which the boy sees as normal and so he would never see any need to mention it to staff. And even were Jimmy worried about his mother's attitude to the affair, he'd hardly be likely to mention the matter to staff as he would implicate himself in a fairly major theft.

Further, being away from home, the boy who does have problems at home is likely to experience them less intensely while at Dalmore. He is no longer in the position of going home every night to what he perceives as an intolerable position; rather he goes home probably two nights in fourteen. When in the house on leave he may find his parents relatively pleased to see him and life in the house may be temporarily more pleasant. Also 'going home' on leave for the boy may mean going to his extended rather than his nuclear family; the houses of various uncles and married brothers may all be part of 'home' where the boy may spend a night or two. 'Home' as the address of the nuclear family may exist only in the files of the various welfare agencies the boy has been processed by. More than this, most of the time on leave may be spent on the streets and for the older Dalmore boy, his nuclear family may be largely past history (Parker 1974:37). Difficulties in the family may be but memory rather than a current 'problem' for him.

Thus the general orientation of the boys militates against their perceiving themselves to have the sort of problems indicated by the official philosophy, and if they do perceive themselves to have such problems they are unlikely to relate them to their being in trouble with the law or to getting out of Dalmore. What kind of problems outside though are boys likely to see as relevant to their stay in Dalmore? These tend to be problems which ensue from, rather than lead to, their stay in Dalmore. Family problems, for instance, may be experienced that were not there before. Although some parents may be glad to have a rather troublesome adolescent out of the way for a few months, others may be anxious about what List D school

71

is doing to their child. As one boy commented on what Dalmore had done for him:

> - ....I suppose it's done no bad. It's made a change trouble-wise. I went to Court. It's made a change that way, but - in other ways it hasnae - being away from home and that, upsetting my ma and my da, it's just caused all that, you know. It's worse to see my ma upset and my da upset. I hate it.

> - Does that cause trouble when you go back home?

> - No, it doesnae cause trouble. It doesnae cause trouble, but my da and my ma - you know, they feel rotten about it. It sometimes causes arguments between them two, you know - thinking about it. They're good parents to me anyway.

Such a problem as this a boy may not see much point in raising since there is not very much can be done about it other than to get out of Dalmore as quickly as possible.

Even if a boy does experience himself as having the kind of 'problems' indicated by the official philosophy, and even if he wants to talk about them, he may find this difficult. He may fear staff probing deeper than he would like into events that are either traumatic or illegal. Or he may find it difficult ensuring that only the right people come to hear of his problem. Since the headmaster spends the day not in an office of his own but in the Board Room in which several other staff may be present, boys who want to see the headmaster alone are often worried that others may also be present and may spend most of a day hanging around trying to find a moment when he is alone. Or a boy may not want other boys to know that he has family or other problems. Or he may fear untoward sanctions: for instance, one boy described to me one December how he wanted to talk to someone about how he wasn't getting on well with his parents but he dared not tell a member of staff for fear of not being allowed out for

72

Christmas leave.

The boys' orientation to discussing family pathology
then, inhibits the production of the kind of information staff need to diagnose their 'problems'. Are
there routine situations in which staff attempt to
elicit such information directly from boys, and is it
more forthcoming in these situations? There are two
such situations - group counselling and interviews
between a boy and his social worker. I will look at
each of these in turn.

GROUP COUNSELLING

Group counselling is timetabled once a week for an hour
or so, on a house basis. According to the headmaster,
group counselling should be largely oriented to the
problems a boy faces on release, and this is a slightly
different emphasis from the 'problems' which lie at the
root of his getting into trouble. The two are related,
though, in that the problems faced on release are seen
as a modified and possibly exacerbated form of earlier
'problems'. Group counselling both teaches staff what
boys' 'problems' are, and enables boys to face up to
them. This has been described by the headmaster as
follows:

> ...The more you counsel, the more you recognise
> the kinds of problems children face going back
> to the community. Their peers are there. They
> are going to have to live with them. They are
> going to have to face up to them. There is no
> way round that. Some of these people will force
> their attention on them. They will expect more
> of them - they are now approved school boys, and
> they will really have to show their paces. You
> have got to face them with these possibilities.
> ...People think that because children are doing
> fine in the school and it's time for them to go
> back that they should just automatically settle
> in. The bloody problems are still there. They
> have got to face them. Maybe even in a more

virulent form...

More specifically, the kind of 'problems' that group
counselling should facilitate discussion of are as
follows:

> Apart from the fact that these children are under-
> privileged, most of them, and that they come from
> unsatisfactory homes, they have more simple
> problems than that - that in fact are never
> considered, that they really don't know how to
> handle or that they think they know how to handle
> and handle them quite wrongly. Being part of a
> gang, for instance, sexual relationships, their
> relationships with the police, going back to
> school, how to handle a problem in the classroom,
> people at school....

To what extent in practice, though, does group counselling succeed in facilitating discussion of boys'
'problems', whether in the family or other areas?
Different staff feel differently about this: one social
worker told me he felt that group counselling was
important in that it enabled boys to think about their
parental situation. I asked him how easy it was to
get boys to discuss their families, and he answered:

> Yes, it's very easy when a discussion's got going;
> just to throw in a question which will really
> get them talking. Something like - how much
> pocket-money do you think you should get? And a
> boy might say straight away, my old man's a
> skinflint, and then they're straight off. Or
> you could ask, how late do you think you should
> be allowed to stay out till at night?

Another social worker told me he felt discussion of
family problems was more difficult to engineer:

> - Well, in group counselling this does happen but
>   it depends a lot on the group. If the group's
>   not very intelligent and they're not very
>   communicative, you can't get a really good

74

discussion going. Very often you get boys who
have been rejected in so many spheres that
they're demanding things all the time. One of
the topics will be food and that will be brought
up week after week. We get a bit tired of it.
Also, members of staff get discussed. But if
you've got a group with a fairly high intell-
igence and able to communicate, they can be
manipulated to bring out various problems at
home. Often you find that if one boy starts
on this theme, then others are prepared to give
vent to their feelings too.

- Is this less more often then that they would
  talk about their families?

- Oh, well, it's less. Their span of concentration
  is low, but if you're lucky you can get a good
  group.

The general feeling of all ranges of staff as expressed
to me is that having group counselling is better than
having no group counselling, but that it is far from
working as the theory says it should.

My own observation of groups indicates that the time
actually allotted to them is often less than the formal
hour. They usually follow housemeetings at which
aspects of the running of the school are discussed and,
if this is not completed on time, group counselling may
be partially or wholly taken over with completing the
housemeeting business. Even when groups do actually
get going, the most usual starting point for discussion
is matters inside rather than outside Dalmore. Often
boys concerned about their comfort rather than about
therapy begin with complaints about the school and
never get off the subject. Some of the teaching and
instructing staff feel groups not to be very helpful
if they become perpetual moaning sessions, especially
if the moaning is about aspects of the school which
such staff are powerless to change.

My impression is that the groups which have operated

75

nearest to theory and in which the boys have shown most
interest have been those in the Cottage. In these
groups, the discussants are those who live with each
other, whereas in the main school the discussants in
any one group do not necessarily see much of each other
for the rest of the week. In the Cottage there is much
more discussion of interactional difficulties between
boys and boys, and between boys and staff, and, indeed,
groups may be held on an ad hoc basis to sort out
fights or other trouble as they occur. Also, the
housemaster knows his boys better than in the houses in
the school and is usually more able to channel the
group into what he sees as a fruitful direction. But
what characterises these groups as against school
groups is that they discuss interactional difficulties
in the Cottage instead of more generalised complaints
about the school. I have no evidence they spend more
time discussing boys' problems outside Dalmore.

How do boys experience group counselling? Boys do
not distinguish group counselling from the housemeetings that deal with the administration of Dalmore. One
boy who did see groups as a separate activity described
it as more or less a free period. He enjoyed talking
about life outside, but it appears that in his experience the discussion often got bogged down in Dalmore
affairs:

  - We dinna do nought, we just sit about. Great,
    man! We get a member of staff like (name of
    teacher), talks like crap an' that. Tells you
    stories and everything. Great! What you do
    on leave and everything. Drugs an' that. Ken,
    talk about things that happen outside an' that.
    Not all this shit about things in the school.
    An' he'll give you fags and sweeties - it's
    great. Or, you dinna' even speak - just read
    newspapers. Books and everything. Great!

  - It's good when you talk about things outside?

  - Aye. But when you're talking about shit about
    the school. Like smoking in the leave bus an'

76

that - it's been discussed hundreds of times
and you discuss it again. The guv should just
say if you smoke in the bus you lose three
leaves, but instead he talks about it. Should
talk about something sensible.

Tutt (1974:78-79) concludes that counselling makes
staff more aware of boys' 'problems', but points to
several inhibiting aspects of groups. For the boy to
portray his family as pathological will considerably
lower his status in the group and may delay release:

> He is very unwilling to give any information
> which may affect his release. From the boy's
> point of view, if he starts talking about problems
> at home...then the staff may well use this inform-
> ation against him by further deferring his release.
> The boy's first aim is to deny the existence of
> all problems since, if he has no problems, he is
> presumably more likely to be released. This is
> a difficult situation to resolve, since inform-
> ation gained from group counselling is likely
> to affect decisions about the boys' treatment.

The main difference between Tutt's view and mine is
that he, at the time a school psychologist and counsellor, presupposes that all approved school boys
actually do have 'problems' and are trying to 'hide'
them, whereas I would prefer to see group counselling
as a conflict situation in which each side attempts to
fill the agenda with their concerns rather than the
other side's. There are maybe several situations in
life in which people might find it appropriate to talk
about their problems; but group counselling in a List
D school is not usually one of them.

INTERVIEWS WITH SOCIAL WORKERS

The social work staff see themselves as being available
for boys to come and talk to. They make clear to new
boys that they, the social workers, should be the first
person a boy should think of going to if they have any

problems.

One social worker told me he was satisfied that boys
felt free enough to come and see him about their problems, although it may be significant that he is seen
by many boys as the most senior of the social workers,
indeed has even been believed (incorrectly) by some to
be the deputy head:

> Here at Dalmore I find I don't need to go and
> sit down and interview boys: they come and talk
> to me. They're not so embarrassed as the older
> boys at (previous school). A boy's prepared to
> tell me or somebody or other, somebody he's
> established a relation with that's good enough
> to enable him to feel he can go and talk with
> them.

Other staff, though, know about boys that don't get to
see their housemaster because they don't trust him or
because he is too busy. As one trade instructor told
me:

> You know, a boy may get a letter from home and
> it may be worrying him and he'll want to talk
> to somebody but his social worker is busy tied
> up for the first three days of the week maybe
> sorting out leave and that kind of thing so
> he's got no-one to talk to about it.

However, even if there is easy access to social
workers, the interviewer still has the basic difficulty of talking about a boy's family when he may have
very little other information available on the family
bar what the boy chooses to tell him, especially since
the creation of local authority social work departments
in 1968 when home visiting was taken out of the hands
of approved schools. As one social worker told me:

> - In my previous school (i.e. pre-1968), I had
>   responsibility for a geographical area so I
>   knew the parents of these boys, I visited the
>   parents, I knew as much about the boy through

78

the parents as I did directly from the boy and
so this made the interview situation easier.

- Well, this produces a difficulty for you,
  doesn't it? How do you get to know about these
  boys' homes now you don't visit the home?

- Yes, well, we have lost a lot of the contact,
  although we do get a lot from the boy himself.
  But it's still not the same as being able to
  casually say to a boy, 'Ah, I saw your ma last
  week and she said she was having trouble with
  that neighbour up the road', or 'I saw Jeannie
  in hospital last week', or 'I hear your sister's
  getting married next week; how do you feel
  about that?' You know, you had something to
  talk about.

This kind of harking back to the good old days is
common among those staff who were on the welfare side
before 1968; these men now feel they have to talk with
a boy about a third party which is perpetually absent
and unable to join in what should be a three-cornered
discussion between staff, boy and parents.

  Most of the social workers say they attempt to interview each new boy that comes into their house in order
to get to know each boy and his situation individually.
This is the only occasion when social workers routinely
aim to interview all their boys. Precise methods of
doing this vary; one man described his routine to me
as follows:

  I like to see boys after they've been here a week
  or so. Not before then - I'd just pass them in
  the corridor and say, 'How are you getting on?'
  But when I interview them I never jump them for
  anything. You know, I'd look up their social
  background report and most of these usually say
  that the boy's problems are at home. You know,
  the boy's been apart from a parent for a long
  time, and this kind of thing. So I'd have a
  friendly chat about how he's getting on in

Dalmore, what his likes are, what his dislikes
are, who he's friendly with, who his halfer is...

By starting the interview with getting to know the boy
as he is in Dalmore rather than immediately asking
about life outside, this man takes a low profile approach to initiating discussion of a boy's family
'problems'. This may take time and there is no simple
formula; indeed the interview may not be seen as the
best situation for the boy to talk about his family:

You've got to work on it. You've just got to
wean the boy along. And maybe, you know, you
have to drag for a wee while. And you might
find that in a sport or a recreation situation
you'd be talking away and then he starts expounding
to you about his family, and this can be a very
valuable time. For example, he might just mention
that he doesn't go to the football with his dad
any more. And you might say, 'Oh, why's that?'
and you'd carry on from there. I would say that
I don't have any given sequence; it would depend
really on the personality of the boy.

Each social worker then has a different approach to
the task of talking with the boys in his house, and
each may adopt different techniques with different boys.
This could account for the fact that I have never heard
boys talk of an interview with their housemaster as
something that all boys routinely have in the few weeks
following admission. In the strict sense of a formal
one-to-one sit-down interview, probably not all boys
are interviewed. Some effort, though, is made by their
housemaster to see them in some manner or other.

INFORMAL CONVERSATIONS WITH OTHER STAFF

Most of the social workers at Dalmore used to be trade
instructors. The informal situations which they say
are more productive of information about a boy's family
are often those where they are working alongside a boy
in a work situation. These social workers often don

their overalls to help out on the maintenance side and
find that this sometimes aids their welfare work.
Sometimes they regret the loss of contact with boys
that their present position as social workers entails,
a view shared by some teachers and instructors:

> You get someone like (names three social workers)
> and they tell a boy to come into their office
> and sit down and they'll tell him, 'Now, tell
> me about your parents', and of course the boy
> clams up and doesn't say anything. There's no
> comparison with when you are out working with a
> boy and it just comes up in the course of con-
> versation.

To what extent do non-social work staff actually
utilise the work situation for such conversation? This
varies considerably depending on the instructor. The
tailoresses, for example, say that the tailor's shop
may be so flooded out with boys who come just to talk
in addition to those who are there to work that they
can't get their work done:

> From 8 to 8.40 in the morning this place is just
> crowded out with boys. They're all lined up
> there against that bench. They just come to see
> us...They come to see us like we're old friends.
> They'll read their letters out to us and tell us
> about their uncles and aunts and what's wrong
> with their home life.

But apart from the tailoresses and one or two other
female staff, the non-social workers do not claim to
see therapeutic conversations about boys' 'problems'
as a major part of their work. Most take a fairly
laissez-faire approach; as one instructor replied to
my asking how often boys talked to him about their
parents:

> Well, it varies, for example. Take Charlie and
> Hugh – they talk a lot, but I think it is wrong
> to quiz these boys. They've been questioned and
> questioned for so damn long. But if it comes out

81

incidentally that's fine.

All grades of staff feel that informal work situations are either not productive of information about boys' families or not as productive as they should be.

Even when such information is forthcoming, instructors often experience blockages in the reporting of such information to higher levels of staff who are more in a position to act on the basis of the information. Instructors say that social workers or the headmaster are sometimes too busy or can't be found, or that reaction from on high to such reportage of information has in the past been unsympathetic so that they now keep the information to themselves. Other instructors, though, say they have good channels of communication upwards. However, since instructors no longer attend the staff meetings in which boys are reviewed, there is no regular occasion on which they are routinely verbally asked for their opinion on a boy. Unless indivually asked by a social worker, the instructor has to seek him out. Further, apart from their monthly reports for gradings meetings, there is rarely any written record by instructors of conversations with boys. Domestic and evening duty supervisory staff in the Cottage sometimes enter notes on such conversations in the files, but such notes are not made in the main school.

The concentration of decision making at the top of the staff hierarchy means that many boys go straight to the headmaster if they want a practical issue sorted out. Every Wednesday evening the headmaster is available to be seen by any boy, and anything from about ten to thirty boys avail themselves of the opportunity each Wednesday. Boys are not barred from knocking on his door at other times, but Wednesday night is a time when boys know he will be available. The headmaster sees this as a valuable time, one of its functions being the discussion with a boy of family and other problems. The headmaster feels that a lot of boys come to discuss their problems with him rather than with someone else because he is the person with most power to solve them:

There are boys who feel that the only person who can help them is me. You know, the social workers are all right, instructors, teachers, fine, you know, they talk about their problems and are able to come to terms with certain aspects of them but they feel nevertheless that I am the man here eventually who is going to make the wheels turn. This is the way they look at it.

This is indeed the way they look at it. The most common reasons boys come to see the headmaster on a Wednesday night are to ask for reinstatement of leave or for extra leave, and to enquire about their release date. Also, fears about their relations with other boys in the school, and requests to be transferred to the Cottage are fairly common. For all of these, the ultimate decision-maker is perceived to be the headmaster. Worries about family or other situations outside the school, however, are not so easily under the control of the headmaster, and these are correspondingly rarer as reasons for going to see him. Thus, although the discussion of family problems does occur, it is by no means typical of consultations between a boy and the headmaster.

In this chapter I have examined the various situations in which boys talk to staff about their 'problems'. The routine and everyday situations such as group counselling, seeing a social worker, informal conversations with other staff, and Wednesday nights, do produce some information but there is no requirement for every boy to speak about his family or about aspects of his life outside that bother him. This situation corresponds with that which Millham et al. (1975:ch.6) found to be common in approved schools. Although they found that more boys would go to staff with problems than is the case in day or private boarding schools, they still concluded that over half the boys failed to find staff approachable with important problems. Millham et al. noted that failing to approach staff with problems was especially correlated with approved schools where not all levels of staff agreed with the school's formal goals and where there

were few staff meetings in which all staff could
communicate together; such features characterise
Dalmore.

5   Information from outside

I shall be a great deal too far off to trouble myself about you: you must manage the best way you can. (Lewis Carroll)

If senior staff cannot routinely elicit from each boy adequate information about his problems, there are several forms of relevant information arriving at Dalmore from outside – from the locales where the official philosophy indicates the boys' problems lie. Is there enough of this information and is it of the right kind to provide the information staff want? There are three kinds of information – 1. that which comes in a boy's file on admission; 2. contacts from agencies during his stay; and 3. contacts from parents.

1.   INFORMATION ARRIVING WITH A BOY

A juvenile court or Children's Hearing that commits a boy to an approved school or List D school is furnished with a social enquiry report (hereafter referred to as an SER) produced by the local authority social work department, an educational report from the boy's school, and a medical report from his doctor. Each of these is in the boy's file as he comes to Dalmore. Of the reports, the SER is the longest and most comprehensive and since it is the only one that regularly concludes with a specific recommendation for disposal it is likely that it is the most influential as regards the decision to send the boy to a List D school. What kinds of explanation do SERs offer for a boy's getting into trouble? What kinds of 'problems' do they locate as instrumental in his delinquency?

The social enquiry report

The SER always begins with basic information, such as

date of birth, religion, grounds for referral to the Children's Hearings, and previous appearances before a hearing. The writer thereafter creates his own headings. The format generally follows a pattern in which under the heading 'Family' is listed the boy's parents and siblings and their marital status, legitimacy, whether they are at school or work, income, and whether they are at home. Then follows usually a brief physical description of the home, e.g. 'well-kept', 'poorly furnished', and of the neighbourhood. Next comes an extended history of the parents' marital relations and biography of the child, often including childhood illnesses. His offending may be discussed, and then the report always concludes with a summary or assessment, and either a recommendation or an apology for being unable to make a definite recommendation.

The most striking aspect of the SER is the amount of space devoted to describing and discussing the boy's family. All of the fifty SERs which I studied devoted more than half of the report to the family, and many considerably more than half. This is in line with the philosophy and organisation of social work in which the family is seen as the basic unit of need (Smith and Harris 1972). Social workers, along with Dalmore staff, tend to hold the philosophy that 'family pathology' is the 'root' cause of delinquency. To make an SER a field social worker is at least expected to visit the home, talk with at least one parent and be generally observant about what he finds in the house. Some social workers refer to the SER as the 'home background report' - to make a social enquiry about a delinquent means an enquiry into his home background.

When the 'social enquirer' knocks on the front door he is searching for family pathology. Whether he finds it or not, the philosophy that 'family pathology leads to delinquency' appears as the background assumption in the writing of the report, and so the philosophy itself is never challenged. Consider the following four modes of reasoning in cases in which the writer could not discover anything very wrong with the family:

1)   If there is nothing amiss in the family it may be argued that their child cannot really be delinquent and that the offence is probably an isolated occurrence which will not happen again, or which the parents will not allow to happen again. This is illustrated in the following, written about a first offence:

> James is obviously very much concerned about the possible consequences of his offence. He expressed remorse for his actions and stated that he did not intend getting into any more trouble. The parents, too, are much concerned and would appear to be well-meaning persons who have the interest of the family at heart. His mother especially seemed to regret having taken up full-time employment, although she feels that as she comes home at 4.30 p.m. each day she'd be there for James coming home from school...

The fact that James has 'good parents' is used to imply that the boy's good intentions may well be carried out. The concern shown by the parents is looked on approvingly and used to minimise the seriousness of the offence. By contrast, where parents do not seem concerned about their son being in trouble, the writer takes this as indicating a very poor prognosis.

2)   However, if a writer wants to maximise the seriousness of the offence and the boy still appears to come from a good home the writer can do so without contradicting the family pathology philosophy. The argument here implies that if delinquents come from bad families then a delinquent who comes from a good family must be doubly bad. If the devil is not in his family, it must be in himself. This is shown, for example, in a report on a first offender who came from a good home but who took a joyride in a bus which ended in over £1,000 worth of damage. The report implies this is very serious and the last paragraph of the report begins:

> Assessment: He is a bright, mannerly kind of boy who has a good home background. This series of

offences is perplexing in that they seem
completely out of character. Nevertheless,
the repetitive and premeditated nature of the
offences is indicative of a lack of social
conscience....

Whereas the offence could have been construed as the
unfortunately serious prank of a normal boy, the family
pathology philosophy is used implicitly to portray the
offence as inexplicable and to suggest that the court
should be concerned about what unpredictable pastime
the boy might engage in next. The offence was
'serious', yet the home is 'good'; the deduction is
then that the court has a very deviant character on
their hands. He is sent away, under a special order
for a minimum of two years, for this his first offence.

3) Another line of argument where no family pathology has been demonstrated is for the writer to say
there really is something amiss in the family which he
has not yet unearthed. If he finds it difficult either
to write off the offence as an isolated prank or to
demonstrate its atrociousness, he may reason that as
the offence cannot be ignored, he needs time to make
further investigations:

Assessment: ....I recommend voluntary supervision
so that we may gain a fuller picture of the
family situation.

4) If family pathology is not obviously present, yet
the writer assumes that it must be or else the boy
would not have become delinquent, the writer may infer
pathology from certain statements from family members.
These statements would be quite innocuous if the hearer
believed all to be well in the family, but can be
construed as further evidence of pathology if the
family is initially assumed to be in difficulties. For
example:

He receives from mother a fairly large amount
of pocket-money as well as other material things.
Mother's explanation of this is that this is to

remove temptation for him to steal but I feel
that this may be in reality an attempt to compensate for family deficiencies.

This argument can become self-amplifying, the reasoning
going as follows: a) assume or infer from other evidence that family pathology is present; b) therefore,
mother is 'in reality attempting to compensate for
family deficiencies'; c) so she is unaware of her own
motives; d) therefore, she has more wrong with her than
just compensating for family deficiencies; she also
lacks insight; e) therefore, there is more pathology
present than that which we began with in a).

These four types of argument, 1-4, suggest that the
family pathology philosophy, the notion that bad homes
lead to delinquency, is an assumption held by SER
writers which structures every report they write,
rather than a model that they empirically test in each
case. In fact, every one of the fifty SERs I studied
assumed at various points the family pathology philosophy. The philosophy is so flexible that the writer
can use it to back up whatever recommendation he wishes
- the four types of reasoning were regularly employed
in the SERs I studied. The boy could be shown to be
responsible or not, i.e. needing to be dealt with
seriously or not, whatever the evidence about family
pathology. The assessment or recommendation does not
follow in a cause and effect way from the existence or
non-existence of family pathology, yet the philosophy
that bad homes lead to bad kids remains intact as it
can be used to argue whatever is required:

	Assessment	
Evidence	Boy is responsible	Boy is not responsible
Family pathology present	As bad homes produce bad kids, the fact this is a bad home shows he is a bad kid.	This kid is not to blame - it's his background.

Family pathology absent	The act is evil. If evil can't be located in the family, it must be in the kid.	The offence must be out of character. As the kid comes from a good home he must be a good kid basically.

The family pathology philosophy is thus legitimated for the reader. Each SER contains a lot of empirical evidence about the family and so the philosophy appears to be backed up by hard facts, even if the evidence shows that the family is a good one. However, in several SERs in which family pathology was claimed to be present, I found it impossible to decipher exactly how this was supposed to lead to the boy's delinquency. In these reports, together with the reports in which family pathology was claimed to be absent or undetected, there was still over half the report devoted to discussing the family so that Dalmore staff when reading it are left with an implicit reaffirmation of their belief that families are important, yet are given little basis on which to know how this particular family is important. Staff indeed often criticise SERs for not being full enough. They often use SERs as a starting point in the formulating of a boy's 'problems', but often SERs can be no more than a starting point. They legitimate the Dalmore philosophy, but often do not provide specific explanations for the boy in question.

Local neighbourhood information. Most SERs make some mention of the neighbourhood in which a boy lives. This usually involves two kinds of statements. The first is the standard of living in the home in relation to that prevalent in the neighbourhood generally, e.g.:

> The house is poorly furnished but this is in keeping with the general standard in the neighbourhood.

The second kind of information concerns the local 'incidence of delinquency' and again the form of wording is fairly standardised:

The dwelling is a three-roomed tenement flat in an area with a rather above average incidence of delinquency.

Very rarely is such information on the neighbourhood expanded on by the writer, and rarely is it related to the boy's specific delinquency. Rather, as in the two examples above, such information is presented as contextual data on the home, rather than as information which in its own right might shed light on the boy's delinquency.

This marked lack of detail concerning the neighbourhood and its relation to the boy is not surprising given the individual and family casework orientation of social work. Although some field social workers have informally become specialists on certain geographical areas of a town, their work constantly leads them to become specialists on certain families rather than on certain areas. They do not have the kind of information on local and teenage subcultures available to the detached youth worker or the American street corner gang worker, or if they do, they do not display it in the SERs that arrive in Dalmore. Given that an SER is based probably on an interview with the parents, possibly supplemented by a separate one with the boy, it is unlikely the writer will learn very much about the culture of neighbourhood teenagers during that time.

A greater awareness of cultural differences sometimes exists with writers from small town or rural settings, but not a greater tolerance. (Where there is tolerance one would not expect the boy to end up in a List D school). An example of intolerance is provided by a report which claims the subject takes his younger brother with him on his delinquent exploits and that the parents do nothing about this:

....The acceptance of offences committed by their sons is difficult to understand. It is, I feel, closely linked to cultural attitudes in the community....

91

This link is not explored further. The summary at the end points not to cultural diversity within the town, but to the deviant practice of the parents:

> I do not feel this lad can respond any better than he has to supervision and I feel that his parents have played a considerable part in allowing their son to develop in the way he has. Their apparent disinterest concerning this latest offence is very worrying....

It is interesting that the offence was one that Dalmore staff tended to justify as a normal adolescent prank. They generally show a greater awareness of diverse cultural life-styles than is shown in SERs. Several reasons could be given: the SERs that make their way into List D files tend to be written when gentler methods than committal to a List D school have 'failed' and tolerance of the boy's activities is at a low ebb, both by the writer and by other local agencies. Further, the field social worker has to cope with the boy and with local interests that demand something be done about him and he may be forced to a decision in line with demands for the protection of property or the maintenance of law and order. List D staff by contrast may watch from afar and can be more detached about, for example, the culture clash between minorities such as tinker folk or immigrants and their more settled hosts.

Cultural or environmental information and explanations of delinquency in terms of peer group or gang pressure, therefore, form a very small part of SERs. Such explanations are, however, much favoured by another important group of people, namely parents, and this will be examined later in the chapter.

The educational report

Second to the SER in terms of space devoted in the file accompanying the boy to Dalmore and in terms of the importance given it by Dalmore staff is the secondary school report. This is often also summarised in the

SER. The picture painted by the school report is usually one of lower than average IQ and even lower educational attainment, disruptive behaviour and frequent truancy. Dalmore staff believe school to be an important area for understanding their boys and often read school reports with some interest.

When discussing a particular boy or the causes of delinquency generally (Chapter 2), staff often incorporate a boy's school experience, usually one of failure, as an integral part of an eclectic theory. In the SER and educational report, however, no such attempt is usually made. The school report refers to educational matters and it is only a few teachers who discuss anything outwith the school in the final open-ended section on 'other observations'. The summary of the school report in the SER is usually in a paragraph of its own which is not related to the rest of the report. Rather than being part of the explanation of why a boy is in trouble, the educational report comes across merely as additional evidence that the boy is in trouble. It indicates that not only has the boy committed offences but his behaviour and/or progress and/or attendance at school is appalling. It renders the boy and his actions more intelligible by showing that the boy is deviant not only with regard to a few offences but also he is deviant seven hours a day, five days a week at school. The educational report, therefore, serves to shift attention away from the offence as deviant onto the offender as deviant.

Furthermore, the report is from a teacher's perspective rather than the boy's perspective: that is, it describes the difficulties teachers have with the boy. (Dalmore staff by contrast are sufficiently far removed from the task of containing the boy in a secondary school setting that they can discuss the difficulties the boy has with his teachers). The following brief extract typifies the impression that the boy's school feel they can do no more for him, that they would be glad to be rid of him for a while:

A confirmed truant...An extremely indifferent

and badly oriented boy...This boy's record of
truancy and persistent lateness is atrocious.
A complete 'drop-out' as far as day school
education is concerned.

In some ways the boy who does attend school may cause
more difficulties for teachers than do those who stay
away:

Here is a real problem in the making - a boy of
below average ability, from a large family with
insufficient parental attention and support.
Aggressive behaviour to others, bullying,
suspected dishonesty, disruptive behaviour in
the school.

He is reported by the remedial teacher to be
responding to special attention and is eager to
improve his work. On the other hand, the general
report is of a thoroughly objectionable boy at
the moment.

A fuller investigation into this boy's situation
seems called for.

Although truancy is not usually the officially listed
offence it is often a strong contributory factor to the
decision to send a boy away. A not extreme example is
that of a boy in court for three charges of theft by
housebreaking, who was excluded from one school, and
then failed to attend fifty three times out of 126 at
the next school before being excluded from there 'for
gross misbehaviour'. The SER concludes:

....At school he seems to have been very disruptive
and he has recently been excluded from a second
secondary school. Under these circumstances and
in view of the serious nature of the offences,
the court may feel that institutional schooling
is called for.

At Dalmore, concern with the boy's previous behaviour
at school may fade into the background in the same kind

94

of way that the details of previous thefts fade, for neither are issues which staff have to handle on a day-to-day basis. Dalmore does not keep in touch with the boy's secondary school and so what happened while he was there tends to fade from view. Nor is truancy seen as a predictor of absconding. There are, though, two aspects of the educational report that are routinely picked up:

1. Dalmore teachers may note basic educational data, such as IQ and achievement in various subjects. One Dalmore teacher who routinely records details from the educational report notes predominantly the educational rather than the behavioural data.

2. When it comes to considering release, because Dalmore staff believe that school difficulties and truancy are integral parts of getting into trouble, they routinely ask boys under school leaving age if they would like to stay on at Dalmore till they can leave for work (Chapter 6). All such boys are asked this, whether or not there is a record of school difficulties. However, if there is such a record, this will often be read to the boy to emphasise how difficult he will find school if he does leave Dalmore. Thus, a boy's performance at school may be crucial both as regards getting him sent away and as regards his length of stay away.

This completes my examination of the main types of information and models of explanation in the file that accompanies a boy to Dalmore. Mainly these have to do with his school and home, but especially his home. Much evidence of family pathology may be produced, but it is not necessarily obvious how this has affected the boy and influenced his behaviour. Consequently, the file does not routinely provide Dalmore staff with the information they require to understand a new boy's problems. This is a situation peculiar neither to Dalmore nor to Scotland. In England (prior to 1969) each boy went through a classifying school before arrival in approved school and the aim of this was to produce detailed assessments of him so that he could be fitted to the appropriate approved school. My little knowledge of the value that staff in the receiving schools placed on these assessments corresponds to Miller's (1968:75) statement that:

> Much material is often collected with no real assessment as to why the anti-social behaviour occurred. Reports from classifying schools do not make clear their understanding of the aetiology of the disturbance in any one individual. It is thus difficult for a receiving school to be sure where help should be attempted.

The same situation, which I have tried to document, faces List D staff today.

I will now look at what further information Dalmore receive during a boy's stay and whether it is adequate for completing the formulation of his 'problems'.

2. INFORMATION FROM SOCIAL WORK DEPARTMENTS

The agency that provides most information by far on a boy's situation outside while he is away is his local social work department (hereafter abbreviated to SWD) which is the equivalent of the social services department in England and Wales. A boy's secondary school never contacts Dalmore, although Dalmore may send it a report if he is to return there. Police often contact Dalmore but only if the boy has been apprehended for some offence and the contact is usually to decide on arrangements for transporting the boy back to Dalmore or to some other place of safety. Reporters to the Children's Panel are in correspondence to arrange Review Hearings, but again the contact is administrative, although Dalmore may send copies of reports to a Reporter for his records.

List D staff see the local social worker as having two functions - to find out what is going on in the home, and to work with the family. He is seen as the link between Dalmore and family. However, there is no

96

occasion, apart from arranging release, on which
Dalmore and the local authority social worker have to
get in touch with each other. Something slightly out
of the ordinary has to happen in order to necessitate
communication. Indeed, there were four boys in my
sample whose files contain no record of any contact
from the social work department to Dalmore; each boy
behaved consistently well in Dalmore, although two,
according to papers at admission, came from very difficult home backgrounds. Indeed, with one of them there
is a special mention in one of the reports to the court
that sent him to Dalmore that his field social worker
was especially wanting to continue working with the
family to prevent the younger children from following
in their older brother's footsteps.

Although cases in which there is no contact are few,
there are many in which contact is still relatively
rare. For example, with the boy in my sample who had
most contacts (twelve), only one contact is documented
in the seven months following completion of the
admission documents, and by this time, of the nine boys
who had come in the same week, four were about to be
released. With the thirty three sample boys, the
average number of recorded contacts from their SWDs
prior to arranging release was only 2.5 per boy, composed of 1.1 letters, 1.3 phone calls, and 0.1 visit by
the social worker to Dalmore. There was wide variation
though, ranging from nought to six contacts per boy.

This amount of contact is seen by Dalmore staff as
far too low. They complain frequently and often
bitterly about social work departments who are 'not
doing their job', and about field social workers that
'we've not heard a peep from for months'. They look back
longingly to the good old days when there were special
after-care officers for the approved schools service
who visited boys' homes and local secondary schools
and arranged employment on release. From the few old
files I have come across dating back to these days it
would appear that these men did feed back information
about the home far more often than is now the case,
and reading these files I got a 'movie' picture of how

the family might be changing over time. I am not in a
position to give well-founded reasons for the present
low level of contact, but the following would seem
plausible:

1) Boys in List D schools are out of sight and therefore out of mind. A field social worker with a mixed
and high caseload will usually give more attention to
crisis cases. Boys in List D schools are therefore at
the bottom of the priority list, unless they come home
on leave and cause trouble or are to be released and
have no home to go to.

2) Dalmore is 100 or more miles away from many boys'
homes. Few field social workers have a whole day spare
to visit Dalmore for a low priority case, unless the
visit can be fitted in with another reason for trav-
elling as far as Dalmore.

3) The reorganisation of local social work has led to
the creation of many senior posts at a time when most
social workers are only fairly recently qualified and
this leads to very quick movements up the professional
ladder. If a field social worker stays in a post for
only a year or two he is going to spend a good deal of
that time opening and closing his caseload of eighty
or so, and not much time may be left for anything else.
This is shown in the following correspondence in which
after the boy has been in Dalmore for seven months and
nothing has been heard from the SWD, Dalmore write to
them saying they feel the boy ought to be released, and
requesting:

   Perhaps you will let me know your feelings on
   this and how the situation is at home.....

The reply begins:

   Miss (..) to whom you wrote has recently left
   the department and Donald's case has now been
   transferred to myself. As I have not yet had
   the opportunity of meeting Donald I think it
   wise for me to remain guided by the views of

yourself.

Hardly a very informative letter for Dalmore (1).

Complaints about social work departments are tact-
fully tempered down if they ever appear on paper. The
following letter sent to the Reporter to a Children's
Panel requesting a Review Hearing for the release of a
boy is an example:

> ...It seems obvious that this boy's problem lies
> in the home and not in the residential situation.
> Only one report has been made by the social work
> department since the boy's admission. This is
> totally inadequate in keeping us abreast of the
> home situation. A letter has been sent to the
> social work department asking for an up-to-date
> report with the view that this boy may be
> released next month......

Dalmore staff feel they get more co-operation from
some local social workers than from others and a few
are seen in a favourable light. These are those that
Dalmore men have built up personal connections with;
such connections may already exist if the local social
worker used to be one of the approved schools' old
after-care officers, or if as part of his training he
came to Dalmore for a placement (so he 'understands the
way we work here'), or if a Dalmore man as part of his
training worked in the other man's department. Thus,
if Dalmore sense they are not getting full value from
a boy's social worker, they may ring up an ex-colleague
working in the same social work department who is often
now a senior field worker and can exercise some lever-
age. Otherwise, if contacts do not already exist,
Dalmore social workers try to build up personal contacts with field workers.

What is most likely to endear a local social worker
to Dalmore staff is if he personally visits Dalmore to
discuss a boy's future with the boy and staff. Such
visits are rare; there is only a record in the files of
three such visits for the whole of the thirty three

boys in the sample (2). However, when such visits do occur there may well be far more information forthcoming and discussed than during the whole of the rest of the boy's stay. The content of what the visitor says, when recorded by myself while note-taking in such encounters, has sometimes extended to more than the sum of all his written reports to Dalmore. Significantly, however, very little of this is written down by the Dalmore staff themselves and an hour's discussion may be recorded by only a brief paragraph in the Occurrence Sheet (a summary in each boy's file of pertinent events). So, although the Dalmore staff who actually met the visitor may memorise a lot of what transpired, this is not available to others in any detail.

Staff often complain about lack of contact with social work departments, but for all practical purposes if they hear nothing from the SWD they assume nothing is amiss in the family. This comes across in file after file in which, if the SER is anything to go by, the boy's committal to a List D school is largely influenced by the perception of the existence of family pathology, and yet little mention of the family is to be found thereafter in the file and he is released with reference to his behaviour in Dalmore rather than to improvement in the family situation. Dalmore staff's normal reasoning became explicit in one incident where, exceptionally, a 'mistake' was made by them and was seen to be made. A letter from the Director of a local SWD arrived a few days after the boy was released.

> I am disappointed that you did not feel it prudent to consult with me before deciding to send Kenneth home. The family are in the midst of a deep crisis at present, with both parents having great difficulty coping with their marital and domestic problems. The father has been drinking excessively and another member of the family is currently in trouble with the police. Kenneth arrived home to a situation of turmoil, when no-one had much time to devote to him. Was it therefore a coincidence that he became involved in the petty fraud and has been charged with this

offence within two days of his homecoming.......

The reply from Dalmore apologises for the omission,
stating that normally the social work department is
informed a month or so before release,

> Nevertheless I am disappointed that such a state
> of affairs should exist in this boy's home and
> us not know about it. Indeed, we have had no home
> report at all from your department and, therefore,
> must under the circumstances feel that <u>unless we
> hear from you nothing is amiss</u>...... (my emphasis)

If there is no word from the social work department,
although Dalmore staff may complain among themselves,
for all practical purposes concerning the boy's career
they have to assume that 'nothing is amiss'.

Trouble during leave

There are exceptions to this. One is when a boy causes
unexpected trouble, especially if the trouble happens
while he is on home leave at a time when all is well
with him inside Dalmore. If a boy is apprehended for
an offence while on leave, this often leads to a re-
definition of the boy and his problems and to requests
to the social work department for additional information. For example, the following boy had been seen to
be progressing for several months and was on the point
of release. Then he was involved in an offence and a
Dalmore social worker wrote to the SWD:

> This lad's recent theft caused us concern and the
> fact that he absconded last week is also most
> disturbing. At Dalmore he is still the pleasant,
> hard-working lad who causes no disciplinary
> problems and <u>so we can only assume that the home
> circumstances are still unfavourable and that the
> lad is subjected, by the environment, to a certain
> degree of emotional distress</u>..... (my emphasis)
> He maintains that his enuresis is as bad as ever
> it was and that the father still spends most of
> his time in the local bar. It would therefore

be appreciated if you could make investigations
as to the parental relations within this home.

This boy's 'problem' had been 'diagnosed' over a year
before as one of anxiety (of which the bed-wetting was
symptomatic) about the parental relations and especially about his father. The boy was considered to have
got over this sufficiently to be released, but the
offence immediately led the writer of this report to
infer that his 'problems' were not solved after all and
so he requested the local social worker to diagnose the
situation further.

Not only does trouble on leave enable a re-diagnosis,
it can also lead to a re-working of treatment. Thus,
with another boy, a very hopeful report to a Review
Children's Hearing stated:

> He moves from strength to strength. The dis-
> appointment at not being released at Easter he
> has borne with fortitude. In the light of such
> maturity, he has been permitted to reside at home
> in the evenings, returning to school at 8 a.m.
> each morning. It is also gratifying that his
> recent Easter leave passed without incident and
> it would seem that he has gained in self-
> confidence..... (my emphasis)

However, a theft three days after this report was
written led to the following letter from the same
author to the SWD:

> His recent theft makes it necessary to re-assess
> his programme of treatment. On the two occasions
> he has been permitted to live at home in the
> evenings he has lacked the strength to keep out
> of mischief.....

I am not suggesting that offences committed during
home leave always lead to the formulation of a boy's
'problems', or always lead to correspondence with the
SWD. Rather, offences are a cue which Dalmore staff
may pick up. Their philosophy is that boys who are in

102

trouble must have 'emotional problems' and so any boy
who comes to Dalmore is assumed to have 'problems'.
However, if he behaves well it is easy to forget that
he is there as a troublemaker, and it is often only if
he causes trouble while at Dalmore - and trouble on
leave can be the worst kind as it involves other
agencies and the public - that they restart investigations into his 'problems'.

Refusing to go home

Staff may also be alerted to 'problems' at home by
another exceptional occurrence - if a boy says he does
not want to go on home leave or be released. The major
concern of each boy is to get out of Dalmore and the
two main ways of doing this are going on leave and
getting released. Staff are fully aware of this, so
when a boy tells staff he doesn't want to get out on
leave or get released, or if he returns from leave in
a distressed state, this immediately indicates to staff
that there are 'problems' outside.

   The way in which the decision of a boy not to go on
leave can dramatically alter the definition of a boy
and bring his 'problems' to light is shown in the
following case. The original SER had mentioned that
the parents had 'difficulty disciplining their son' and
that he had been in a children's home for three years,
but otherwise it had not dwelt on specific family pathology. But a report written by his housemaster several
months after his admission to Dalmore construes family
pathology as the defining characteristic of the boy.
It was his refusal to go home which set off this new
definition:

> Relationships in the home clearly manifested
> themselves on Alan's first home leave in that
> he returned to school four days early. Since
> then, Alan has refused weekend leave and
> Christmas leave, being the only boy who wished
> to spend Christmas in school. The lad has
> suffered complete rejection.....

In another case where Dalmore increasingly focussed
upon 'problems' at home even though there was little or
no indication of these in the SER, the cue that staff
went on was a little less obvious. The SER writer had
known the family for two years and described the
parents in unusually glowing terms - they were struggl-
ing to pay a mortgage which was difficult due to a
depression in the father's trade. They had changed
jobs in order to be with the children and despite many
trials and tribulations from the boy 'they have tried
and it is to their credit they have persevered so
long'. Six months later the Cottage Occurrence Book
started recording in exceptional detail all kinds of
out-of-the-ordinary happenings. One Sunday night, the
boy came back from leave 'in a very weepy state' and
the housemaster started talking with him and it transpired there had been quarrels at home with his father
coming home drunk. The housemaster got in touch with
the social work department to find out what was wrong
and reports came back of financial difficulties involving eviction from the house because of non-payment of
mortgage repayments. Over the next thirteen months the
correlation between the boy's behaviour in Dalmore and
the home circumstances was 'confirmed'. The final
review report selected from the Occurrence Book to show
how his behaviour fluctuated with conditions at home
and concluded:

> It is to us therefore obvious that his problem
> is in his home and that his anti-social acts
> are a direct result of unsatisfactory home
> conditions and the lack of any sense of per-
> manency in respect of living conditions.

When a boy does not want to be released to his
nuclear family, Dalmore want to make sure they have
got the facts right before they go to the considerable
bother of finding alternative accommodation for him.
They may want confirmation or amplification of the
story the boy himself gives and so they may try and get
the parents themselves to Dalmore or at least ask the
social work department to visit the home, as requested
for example in this letter from Dalmore:

Edward asked me as his School Welfare Officer
to see him only yesterday concerning his home
leave. He alleged that he had had an argument
with his mother. This as far as I can gather
was over some minor incident involving his sister
but being used by both to gain their own ends.
The issue now is that Edward wants to find digs
and work here (i.e. the area in which Dalmore is
situated). This we are considering at present,
but only in the work sense. We would want to be
sure of Edward before considering digs. If you
should be in the neighbourhood perhaps you would
be good enough to assess the situation at that
end.

If, then, a boy says he does not want to go home,
this almost guarantees investigation by Dalmore and the
SWD into discovering exactly what is the 'problem' at
home. It is, however, very much the exception rather
than the rule that a boy declares unwillingness to go
home, and it is precisely because it is so exceptional
that staff take so much notice when it happens.

3. INFORMATION FROM PARENTS

If information coming from Social Work Departments is,
and is felt by staff to be, inadequate for providing a
picture of a boy's situation outside and the problems
he faces there, information coming direct from parents,
by-passing SWDs, is less frequent still. For a boy in
the sample, the chances were that staff would barely
have one communication (letter, phone call or visit)
from his parents to them during his stay that they
deemed worth recording, and rather less that staff
would correspond with parents. Letters between parents
and their children are much more frequent and are read
by staff, but they are not routinely recorded.

I will now look at each of the types of contact with
parents to see what kind of information they produce
and what kind of models or explanations of delinquency
parents present to Dalmore.

The only routine contact in which every parent has to
supply information comes at the beginning of a boy's
stay when they are asked to forward his medical card
and to fill in a form. These forms are not systemat-
ically consulted by staff for any purpose, and no
decisions are routinely made on the basis of them. The
instructions at the top of the form introduce the parents to the language used at Dalmore - terms such as
'help', 'understand his problem' - and to the pervasive
Dalmore assumption that even before they have met a boy
he has 'problems':

> In order to help your son as much as we can, we
> would like to know more about him. It would
> enable us to understand his problems better if
> you would answer the following questions carefully.

Given that the parents may still be distressed and
anxious about their son's removal from home at this
early stage, these instructions may well motivate many
parents to fill in the form with some consideration.
So, although it may not be put to regular use by staff,
it provides as useful an indicator as I can get from
within Dalmore of the range of definitions of the
situation given by parents regarding their son's getting into trouble. There is only one question which is
consistently answered from one form to another - 'Did
he have companions of whom you did not approve?' Almost
all the parents answer yes to this. Light is shed on
this by answers to another question, 'In what ways did
he worry you at home?' Answers frequently concern
activities <u>outside</u> the home:

- We lived in a rough area, he got in with rough
  boys and started getting in trouble rather than
  be made fun of. He is very easily led.

- pals he kept

- not going to school

- staying away from home.

And rather less frequently, activities inside the home:

- kept the children going. Break their tempers
  and start arguing.

- smoking and not doing what he was told by
  his father.

- when he fractured his skull as a baby, a small
  part of his brain was damaged...

Only once did I come across any indication that the
parents thought they may have been partly to blame:

- His relationship with his step-father was
  very bad and he would not stay at home unless
  I was there.

Apart from this one instance, the only statements that
could be construed as explanations of why their boy got
into trouble as opposed to descriptions of how he got
into trouble were those concerning his 'pals'. Thus,
parents do not hold the 'family pathology' explanation,
and the only explanation they do offer, i.e. bad comp-
anionship in a bad neighbourhood, is one that is per-
sistently ignored by SER writers. Their offering of
this explanation has been noted by the headmaster when
describing counselling groups with families that he ran
before coming to Dalmore:

At first each parent would say their child wasn't
really bad, it was the pals he went about with.
Of course, the group soon began to realise that
everyone was saying the same thing and they then
began to talk more realistically about their boys
and about themselves.

This quotation is typical of staff's attitude in that
it discounts the parents' model of 'It's the other
boys' and reasserts a family pathology model. It seems
to me that even if all parents think it's somebody else
not their Jimmy that's to blame, their model would
still be tenable if one adopted a 'comedy of errors'

theory in which each boy believes the others to be
committed to delinquency but is not committed himself
(Matza 1964) or a theory in which originally innocent
play in some street groups is increasingly and selectively defined as deviant by the authorities while, for
contingent reasons, other groups do not get so defined
(Tannenbaum 1938). Such adaptations of the parents'
model, however, are not attempted by Dalmore staff.
Rather, the apparent falsity of the parents' model is
taken as evidence of their lack of insight which may
in turn be taken as further evidence of family
pathology.

The one exception I discovered was once when Dalmore
were in an unusually strong position to do something
about the other boy who in this instance was named by
the parents. After their boy had been in Dalmore for
a while, the parents complained that their boy was
being led astray while on leave by a boy from another
List D school who got leave the same weekends. Dalmore
arranged with the other school to send the two boys
home on alternate weekends. That this administrative
arrangement was carried out so smoothly was possible
because there are informal channels of communication
between List D headmasters, and because the arrangement
implied neither school had mishandled the case and so
maintained the reputation of both. Normally, however,
neither Dalmore nor social work departments are able to
affect local patterns of association among boys (3).

The regular discounting of parental accounts indicates the low status of parents as seen by social work
departments and by Dalmore. Parents do not wield
financial power over the school (although a few pay a
nominal amount), nor is it easy for them to withdraw
their boy from the school. It is indicative of their
low status that parents are not given the chance to
consult their boy's file except when selected passages
are shown them at the instigation of staff, as is
indeed the case in schools of any description (Goslin
and Bordier 1969:56-57). This does not imply that the
parents are held morally to blame for their child's
being in trouble or that staff do not feel sympathetic.

Just as the children are seen in the treatment model as in need of 'help' rather than 'punishment', so too are their parents:

> In most cases parents are anxious to help and looking for help. Their experiences generally had perplexed and worried them and, contrary to what many people think, they are deeply concerned about their son's welfare. The situation has got beyond their control and, because of their own background or their own training, or perhaps limited intelligence, they were ill-equipped and quite unable to deal with it. (headmaster)

Complaints about other boys

Given that the predominant explanation held by parents is that their child is in trouble because he's been led astray by bad company, it is not surprising that they should fear for their boy when he is sent to a List D school containing ninety-nine other boys who, according to the parents' theory, are all worse than their boy and are bad company for him. One type of contact from parents to Dalmore, then, consists of complaints about their boy being bullied or terrorised by other boys in the school. The following kind of letter occasionally arrives at Dalmore:

> I hope you don't mind me writing to you, but Jamie was awful down in the mouth when he was home on leave and he was on the verge of crying when he was due to go back so I forced him into telling me what was wrong with him and he said he didn't want to tell but other boys were bullying him all the time and hitting him...
> He's such a great wee chap in the house and he fair likes all the people who are in charge of him, but I hate to see him like this. I said, do you want Mum to write and explain. He got awful upset and said, Oh, no, I don't want to cause any bother as they're awful good to me. But after thinking it over I was afraid he might run away and that would be worse than me writing

109

you, so I will leave it to you as you will know
what best to do. Very sorry for troubling you
like this as we are so grateful for all you have
done to help him as it is and he is a very mixed-up
little boy but so willing to try hard.

The reply to the letter is typical in that it denies
that bullying is going on:

Thank you for your letter of the 5th and it is
indicative as to how your boy uses the world
to satisfy his own desires or to gain or invoke
sympathy. We have investigated this matter
regarding bullying and apart from the usual
differences between boys there is no foundation
to his story....

The refusal to agree with parents' allegations that the
company at Dalmore is bad for their boy is shown most
acutely in the following incident in which a boy failed
to return from leave. At the resulting Boys' Hearing,
one of the Dalmore social workers stated:

Charlie's mum was on the phone to us saying
that Charlie was not wanting to come back
because he was frightened of gangs in the
school. I told her that there weren't any
gangs in the school but if there were any
forming we'd break them up. She said could
she come up and discuss it - she was obviously
very concerned.

The previous day, however, the senior staff had been
discussing among themselves what to do about a particularly strong clique of boys that was developing. In
reply to this same social worker, the headmaster had
admitted:

You know, this is the nearest to a real gang
we've had here in the school for five years.

Dalmore staff discount parents' explanations that
'it's the other boys' both when it is boys outside

Dalmore and boys inside that the parents are referring
to. Such allegations may easily be turned back on
parents to show they 'lack insight' or on the boy to
show he is 'manipulative' or 'uses the world to satisfy
his own desires'. They are not used as cues for the
staff to elicit further information from parents on the
peer group pressures on the boy.

Other complaints

Another type of complaint from parents may produce
similar counter-allegations by staff against parents or
boy and this is when there are complaints about the
handling by staff of the boy. Such complaints are very
rare, but the following case illustrates what can
happen in that, although the boys' parents pulled off
the difficult feat of getting him out of Dalmore, they
earned an unfavourable definition from the staff in the
process. Gordon had absconded and on being apprehended
eighty miles from Dalmore was placed for the night in
a local remand home. The Occurrence Sheet records for
that day:

> Phone call from Gordon's mother. Very upset
> about not being told about her boy being in a
> remand home and she is going to see her MP.
> She insists that we should release the boy
> immediately and I informed her that this was
> not within our power and that she would have
> to make request to her local Reporter for a
> Hearing if she wanted Gordon to be returned to
> her.

Any boy in a List D school, or his parents, are entitled to ask for a Review Hearing after three months
and once every six months thereafter, but this happens
very rarely. The Hearings, sixteen days later, released Gordon, despite a review report from Dalmore
which recommended he stay in a List D school for
another year until old enough to work and which
described the parents in these terms:

> ...(it is) obvious that neither Gordon nor his

111

parents seem capable of responding to the
counselling and treatment provided by us.
The fact that the parents have requested this
hearing shows that they will pursue their
assessment of Gordon's readiness to be released
to return to day school. It is at an emotional
level discounting advice given as to their boy's
needs. Their over-indulgent attitude which is
the root cause of their son's difficulties is
conclusive.

If the parents complain about their boy rather than
Dalmore this can still be turned back on them and
construed as evidence that they are 'inadequate'. One
family which was seen by the social work department as
scapegoating their son was frequently visited by the
local social worker who often wrote to Dalmore of their
'defensiveness' and 'unwillingness to look at their own
difficulties which they are projecting onto their son'.
Dalmore staff were pleased with the unusual amount of
time and effort this field social worker was putting
in.

Complaints from parents as recorded in the files are
rare but they are revealing in that they show that
Dalmore can construe 'family pathology' out of what
the parents themselves define as parental concern for
their boy. Staff were aware in these instances that
the parents were concerned, but saw this as misguided
concern. In all these cases staff had other kinds of
evidence not mentioned here to indicate family pathology and the subsequent parental communications were
used to confirm already emerging deviant identities
for these families (4).

Requests

Parents may also contact the school with various
requests, usually about leave or illness and occasionally about release. A request may often be met in its
own terms and there may be no overt using of the
request to demonstrate the character of the parents.
Such is usually the case with requests for extra

leave to enable a boy to attend the wedding of a close relative. Goffman (1968:75) and Tutt (1974:94) suggest that relatives often do not have enough contact with an institution to learn what constitutes a valid request and consequently many requests are rejected by the institution as inappropriate. At Dalmore, though, it seems that it is complaints rather than requests which generally backfire on relatives.

Enquiries about normal leave may demonstrate to staff that the parents are 'concerned'. For example, one boy was being kept by an elderly grandmother who after three months wrote to ask if she could have some help with his bus fare to and from leave. This evoked a very sympathetic reply which spoke of being 'impressed' by her efforts to get the money to pay the fare, agreed to pay the fare in future and reimbursed her for her past expenses.

Another boy living with his grandfather was the subject of some rather more heated letters. This one from the grandfather was typical of five:

> Sir,
> I do not want Harry home this weekend. I had a visit from (the local social worker) and I understand that Harry was not to be home for a few weeks until Christmas when he would be home for a fortnight's leave so I do not want him to be sent home every weekend. I hope I make myself clear.

Replies from Dalmore say that it would be a pity if Harry did not get leave every week or two like the other boys and Harry would be quite upset. Eventually the matter seems resolved when the school sent the grandfather maintenance money for the boy. There is no mention by the school in connection with this correspondence that the grandfather is rejecting the boy.

Contact from parents regarding release may also be dealt with in a similar matter-of-fact way. Parents who write saying they have arranged employment for

their son may succeed in speeding up release by a few
days:

> I was asking Brian when he was expecting to get
> released and he told me to write a note to you.
> Well, I can definitely say that Brian has a job
> with my firm as a bricklayer or joiner, the job
> is whatever he wants. He will start work after
> the annual holiday on July 14th. The firm is
> (name). Thank you for the change in our son in
> the last two - three months.

Brian was released in time to start this job, slightly
prior to some of his contemporaries who were also due
for release.

Letters to children

Letters from parents to their boy or vice-versa are
read and, although not quoted in reports, may provide
some basis for Dalmore's emerging picture of the
parents. News of brothers and sisters in trouble or
doing well may be used as evidence of pressures within
the family. Parcels may also be used as evidence, as
in the following report which cites them as evidence
of 'over-indulgence':

> He is a very talkative, hyperactive boy who has
> been over-indulged by his parents...They still
> send the boy parcels of sweets which are rationed
> and controlled, or he would just sit down and
> eat the lot. They have been spoken to regarding
> these parcels but still continue to send them,
> although in other respects they are anxious to
> co-operate and have visited the school on a
> number of occasions.

It would seem that with parcels, as with leaves, the
average that most boys receive is seen as a 'reasonable'
amount. Parents who want fewer leaves or send many
more parcels are creating inequalities among boys, and
staff are concerned to try to level these up. Such
concerns may be expressed by labelling the parents as,

114

for example, 'over-indulgent', but such labelling is
by no means a necessary outcome especially if there is
no other confirmatory evidence. In the parcels case
the boy had been seen as 'indulged' for some time
previously.

Visits

Contact is sometimes face to face, for parents sometimes come to the school for a discussion with the
headmaster and social work staff. These discussions
are not recorded in the files, except occasionally.
The following is the longest record that I found, and
it indicates that this particular face-to-face
encounter produced a rather more vivid picture of the
family than had been hitherto gained from written
reports by the social work department:

> Lad's mother, brother and mother's 'friend'
> (male) visited this afternoon. Mother is a
> glib talker, obviously used to putting on an
> act for other social agencies. She is an
> unattractive lump of a woman who keeps trying
> to demonstrate what a good mother she is.
> Some of her statements failed to agree with the
> SW's report and her conversation was larded with
> euphemisms. Brother is a weedy-looking
> character who had nothing to say apart from
> an occasional exhortation to the lad to be a
> good boy. The friend just sat, smiled and
> clicked his teeth. He looked something of a
> simpleton, as he would have to be to be a
> friend of Mrs (...)....His sole attempt at
> conversation consisted of - 'Isn't it time we
> were away, Val'. A most unimpressive trio. It
> is little wonder that the lad has given so much
> trouble in the past.

Since most visits, though, are not recorded, not all
interested staff may hear of the visit and, if they do,
they may not have time to hear the whole story. Visits
by parents may be referred to later in progress and
review reports, but this is often the only written

record of the important decisions about a boy which may be made during or as a result of the visit.

Visits by parents, though, are rare. One reason for this may be that boys go home on leave every week or every fortnight. It is unlikely that parents (usually with low incomes and often with large families) would travel 100 miles to see their son one weekend if he is coming home on leave the next. Similarly, letters from parents to their sons may be less frequent than they would be if leave were rarer. Gill's (1974:94-99) account of Whitegate approved school indicates that leave is less frequent there but that visits and letters from parents are common. Thus, although frequent leave increases contact between parents and boy, it may radically decrease contact between parents and staff.

The cessation of the old system whereby the approved schools had their own after-care staff has led to a drastic reduction in home visiting by List D staff, although parents are occasionally seen at home or at Review Hearings. Visiting of parents by staff is even rarer than visits to Dalmore by parents.

Senior staff feel that they should see a lot more of parents. There are frequent pleas among staff 'to get the parents themselves down here' since there is in their view no substitute for this, and regularity of the pleas demonstrates the difficulties staff face in getting information from and about boys' families. This was demonstrated by one Dalmore social worker who talked to me in unusual depth one day about the 'problems' one particular boy had with feelings of insecurity about his father who recurrently beat the mother. The whole story had come out when the mother, who lived locally, had come up to Dalmore the previous week. But the social worker ended his account to me with:

> ...The boy's local social worker hadn't found any of this out. It could have been months before we found out if the boy's home wasn't

in our local area.

This illustrates how much more detailed staff's knowledge of a boy's 'problems' at home are when parents come to visit, but also how rare it is for this to happen. By implication the amount of information they have on most boys' families is woefully inadequate for their purposes.

CONCLUSION

The official philosophy at Dalmore indicates that each boy has problems and that these lie or originate in his situation outside, especially his family situation. In this chapter I have examined the information about such situations which flows into Dalmore and concluded that this is generally insufficient for the formulation of specific problems for each boy.

1. The social enquiry report accompanying the boy to Dalmore usually assumes a family pathology explanation of delinquency in general but does not always provide enough information to show how such an explanation works with the particular boy. This helps legitimate the philosophy without enabling staff to operationalise it. Other models of explanation take markedly second place in the SER.

2. Other information coming from social work departments during a boy's stay is rare and usually deemed by staff as less than adequate, and this situation seems typical of other List D and community schools Millham et al. 1975:258-61). Adequate information may only be produced on the off chance of the boy getting into trouble while on leave or refusing to go home.

3. Information coming direct from parents is rarer still. Parents do not generally hold the family pathology model of delinquency, but what little contact there is with them may be turned by Dalmore staff into evidence of family pathology.

Indeed, out of three files of sample boys, as many as seven contained no correspondence between admission arrangements and release arrangements apart from a small amount of administration - over leave money (twice), illness (once), extra leave for a wedding (once) and a funeral (once). Consequently, in these files (and in others in the sample too) there is no chance of a diagnosis of the boy's 'problems' being recorded.

All grades of staff feel that not enough is known about boys' homes, either from the boys themselves or from other sources. The following report written about a boy on his release is not untypical in that it admits that no more is known about the home than when the boy was admitted:

> It is not known if any improvement within the home has been accomplished during the boy's period here. There has, however, been considerable improvement in his own personality development.....

In the absence of contact with the home, Dalmore has only the boy himself to work on and to judge improvement by and no staff see this as satisfactory. This then is the fundamental dilemma for Dalmore staff - how to operationalise a philosophy mandating them to help cope with boys' problems when these problems are located outside Dalmore, when communications with outside agencies are poor, and when the boy himself has not learned to relate his 'problems' to his being in trouble. As the headmaster said to me, with some feeling:

> One of the greatest problems is that you cannot control that which you are not involved in. I can't change the situation in a boy's home..... I want somehow to be involved with the family. I mean, I can't expect any more than that at the moment.

NOTES

(1) It is only fair to note that the level of contact
the other way, i.e. from Dalmore to SWDs, is not much
higher. Dalmore write more reports, but make fewer
phone calls.

(2) Again it is maybe fair to point out there is no
record of Dalmore staff ever visiting the local
authority man at <u>his</u> place of work.

(3) It has been suggested to me that List D schools,
in conjunction with courts, could in fact drastically
change gang structures if they made a systematic policy
of incarcerating the leaders of local gangs and keeping
them in List D schools for the maximum three years.
Such a policy will not be implemented so long as family
pathology is the reigning model of delinquency and
delinquent subculture models remain in the background.

(4) It may be the more respectable parents who tend to
be horrified about the company in a List D school, who
are more likely to know how to go about challenging
bureaucracies and large institutions and who therefore
complain and consequently earn a negative standing in
staff eyes. Other families, seen by local agencies as
problem families, may never get in touch with Dalmore
and so long as neither boy nor social work department
bring them into the limelight their contact with the
school may be minimal. Consequently, the perceptions
of a family held by an SWD and a List D school may
differ.

6   Ready for release

'I was thinking', Alice said very politely,
'which is the best way out of this wood?...
Would you tell me please?' (Lewis Carroll)

Getting released is the most important concern of the
boys, and so the criteria on which release is granted
are important in moulding their view of what Dalmore
is all about. How is it decided when a boy should be
released? Does it depend on his good behaviour in
Dalmore or on the resolution of problems at home and
in his local community? Or are neither of these criteria important for release? What criteria does the
boy see as important? How do his concerns about the
timing of release relate to staff concerns? Does his
definition of release affect the timing of release?

RELEASE FROM LIST D SCHOOLS

During the period of research, two laws came into
effect which affected the process of release. One was
the raising of the school leaving age (ROSLA) on September 1st, 1972 from fifteen to sixteen. The effect of
ROSLA will emerge later in the chapter; suffice it to
say now that in this chapter I am referring largely to
the pre-ROSLA era, and data from the post-ROSLA era is
used mainly only to highlight features of the earlier
system.

   The other law was Part Three of the Social Work
(Scotland) Act. Before April 1971, the managers of an
approved school were responsible for the release of
boys, although in practice, they often delegated this
to the headmaster. Officially, the boys were not
released but licensed, that is, returned to the community on licence from, or supervised by, the school
for a period of two years during which they could be

recalled to stay in the school without a further court order. In the present system, the requirement to reside in a List D school may be reviewed by a Hearing of the Children's Panel at the request of the Reporter, social work department, List D school, the boy, or his parents.

Power to release boys from List D schools was not transferred to the panels till June 1971. Thereafter, for several months there was a period of flux in which some panels preferred the schools to release a boy, some held a Review Hearing but followed the school's recommendation very closely, and a few held Reviews without feeling bound to follow the school's recommendation. It was during this transitional period that the boys in my sample were released. In all cases bar one, it was Dalmore that effectively made the decision although the boys usually attended a Review Hearing and the administrative complexity of arranging a Hearing often meant a delay of a few weeks in the timing of a release.

RELEASE FROM DALMORE

Although social work departments, parents, or the boy himself may request a Review Hearing, it is almost always Dalmore that in practice requests one, although there is often negotiation between Dalmore and the Reporter or the social work department as to the timing of the Review. Moves by parents to get their boy released are rare, and when attempted may be resisted by Dalmore if they do not fit in with the staff's views. Requests from social work departments are also rare, and this is in line with the generally low level of contacts initiated by them throughout a boy's stay (Chapter 5). The decision to release a boy or to request a Hearing with a view to release is largely a decision taken in Dalmore.

There is no one specific occasion on which release decisions are made. Discussion about release is frequent during the monthly assessment meetings, and

121

in more informal conversations between the headmaster and Dalmore social workers. Such discussions are often preceded and followed by contacts with the Reporter and social work department, and also with the boy himself, and decisions are often made during such contacts. A common time for boys to discuss their release is on a Wednesday night when they come to see the headmaster, and also at other times when they see their Dalmore social worker. In all cases, though, the headmaster is the final decision-maker. As with admissions where the headmaster feels responsible to his staff and boys who he lets into Dalmore, so with release it is he who is responsible to outside agencies who is let out. This was highlighted during one summer month in which seven boys had been led to believe they would be released and, as their dates drew near, were a little disturbed to be told, 'no boys will be licensed this month as the headmaster is on holiday'.

There are five criteria used by senior staff in discussing whether a boy should be released: 1) the boy should have completed his grades; 2) he should have been in six months; 3) he should have reached school leaving age; 4) his behaviour should be deemed satisfactory; 5) no other 'problems' should be perceived to exist. Every boy who meets all these five criteria is released straightaway; any boy who meets none of the criteria is not released; those who meet some of the criteria may or may not be released. Which, though of the five are the most important? I will look at each of these in turn to try and answer this question.

1. GRADE FIVE

Every month, all the boys are assessed by the senior staff and allocated a 'grade', starting off in grade one and progressing to grade five. It is generally believed that a boy has to have reached grade five before he can be released, and indeed only six per cent of 117 consecutive admissions whose grading careers I studied were released before reaching grade five. It is thus a virtual prerequisite that grade five be

122

reached in order to get released; it is this tying of
the grading system to the boys' major concern of getting released that makes the system important and
meaningful to them. If getting released depends on
reaching grade five, then what does reaching grade five
depend on? Observation of the monthly assessment meetings at which grades are decided showed that going up
a grade each month routinely depends on the boys behaving well, not on whether their personal problems are
being solved. Several reasons can be suggested for
this. It may take a long time for a boy's problem to
emerge, indeed it might never emerge, but in the mean-
time staff feel that he needs some encouragement that
he is not going to be stuck in Dalmore for ever; the
grading system is often justified in terms of giving
boys this encouragement and reassurance. Also, a boy's
problem may reside within his home as much as within
himself, and it would be unjust were he to be penalised
by being kept down in his grades simply because other
agencies were not making progress in sorting out his
family problems. Further, some problems that boys
might have could be personally embarrassing were they
made public to other boys; to base a grading system,
which is inevitably public among the boys, on the
resolution of such problems would necessarily destroy
confidentiality. To sum up, to say that grade five is
a prerequisite for release usually means that good
behaviour is a prerequisite for release.

2. SIX MONTHS

Under the old approved school system, six months was
the legal minimum length of stay. The grading system
at Dalmore was tied in to this - if boys were progressing satisfactorily they should go up one grade each
month so that once in grade five there would be a month
or so to spare to arrange release and then they could
be out in six months. Since each month about eighty
per cent of boys do in fact go up a grade, a considerable number are eligible to get out in six months. Of
the 117 admissions analysed, twenty seven got released
in six months, and the rest at various times there-

after. As the headmaster explained to me:

> If a child can be let away in six months then
> he really should go away in six months. There
> is no reason why he should be kept one minute
> longer. In fact, I was speaking just now before
> you came in about this very thing and saying
> that I would have to send this boy home and even
> if we were wrong he would have to get his chance...
> because he had been really an excellent human
> being while he was here and there was no reason
> in this world why he should be kept one single
> minute longer than was necessary. Now there are
> many children like this.

The boy is led to believe that providing he performs
all right then once he has done six months he is
entitled to go. Many are told the day they come in by
social work staff that 'if you keep your nose clean,
you'll be out in six months to the day', and consequently, boys talk of 'I've done my six months'. It is
often not six months to the day, however, as there may
be administrative delays especially if a Children's
Panel has to be arranged. Of the twelve boys in the
sample who went 1-2-3-4-5 through the grades without a
break and who should have been out in six months, the
average length of stay was in fact six months twenty
days, only four getting out in six months to the day.

The extent to which the six month minimum had per-
vaded the structure of Dalmore was shown when the legal
minimum was reduced to three months. According to the
view of the headmaster quoted above that a boy should
be entitled to go as soon as the legal minimum is
satisfied, we might expect a considerable number of
boys to be getting out in three months now this has
become the legal minimum. In fact, this is not the
case. There is a trickle of boys out now in under six
months, but three months has not replaced six months as
the target. The headmaster gave the following account
two years after the legal change, when I asked how
many Review Hearings he had called for after three
months:

This has happened occasionally and once or twice
the boy has been released as a result, but, you
know, most parents are relieved when one of their
boys get sent away. There might be a lot of
wailing and gnashing of teeth at the time, but
then they discover the pressures are off and
this gives them a chance to look around and see
what the situation is, for the first time in
their lives maybe. Also, think of the local
social worker. He's concerned with his caseload,
with whether he's going to be moving to a new
post. He's concerned about the feelings of the
community, the courts, the police, and the panel
about having a troublemaker back so soon. You
know, I think six months is necessary for most
boys anyway.

So, whether because of institutional inertia or a
revision of the philosophy, or both, the changing of
the legal minimum has not reduced the six month working
minimum at Dalmore.

Boys who have reached grade five and are approaching
six months in the school consequently feel they have a
right to be released, indeed they are usually told
they have a right to be released. However, two months
after having reached grade five, by which time each
boy will certainly have done six months and most administrative delays sorted out, only a minority of boys
(thirty six per cent of seventy two consecutive
admissions November 1970 - September 1971) have
actually been released. This is accounted for largely
by the third main consideration for release:

3. SCHOOL LEAVING AGE

The thirty six per cent of boys who left Dalmore within
two months of reaching grade five were composed of two
very different groups - those who had reached school
leaving age and those who had not. Within two months
of reaching grade five, seventy six per cent of those
over fifteen but only fifteen per cent of those under

125

fifteen were licensed. The average length of stay in grade five of the under-fifteens was 5.6 months - three times that of the over-fifteens.

So if a boy has reached both grade five and school leaving age the chances of his being released are very high. If he has fixed up employment while on leave through relatives, this may speed up release by a few days, but by far the most important factor is his date of birth. Boys are not normally released on their fifteenth birthday but at the Christmas, Easter or Summer holidays following, depending on his local education authority's dates for allowing boys to leave school. Consequently, considerable effort may be spent pressing a local authority which does not have, say, an Easter leaving date on behalf of a boy with a birthday on March 13th who does not want to go back to secondary school and who will have to stay in Dalmore till July whereas had he lived in another area he could be released to employment within a week or two at Easter. These two arbitrary dates - his date of birth and his local school leaving dates - may be the most important determinants of his length of stay.

Why do boys who have not reached school leaving age stay longer before getting released? Some of the reasons typically presented by senior staff are given in the following introductory talk to new boys by the headmaster. At the end he said:

Head: Are there any questions?
Boy: Can I go back to outside school after I've done my six months?
Head: Yes, you get yourself ready to go as soon as possible. But there's a lot of boys don't want to go back. Why's that, do you think?
Boy: Because they don't like school?
Head: Yes, and because they truant and then they get into trouble. And sometimes people expect you to get into trouble if you've been in a place like here, and that makes you get into trouble. It's a hard fact

126

                    but it's true. You must think about that.
                    But no-one will stop you going back to
                    school if that's what you really want.

The reasoning here appeals to the theory that classroom
difficulties lead to truancy and truancy is associated
with getting into trouble. In addition the 'approved
school boy' label may well aggravate classroom difficulties with both pupils and school-teachers such that
the Dalmore boy who found school difficult before he
was sent away will find it even more difficult on his
release. This theory of why boys should not go back
to school is complemented by a theory as to how they
they should come to stay on at Dalmore. The key idea
here is that the boy himself must decide to stay on;
if he is kept against his will after he has 'proved'
himself by completing the grades he will not feel
happy in himself, but a boy who is staying of his own
will will usually cope, given some help, and often
becomes one of the best boys in the school; for some
boys it is not easy, and the key is not to coerce
them. These ideas are, for example, illustrated in the
following discussion with trainee Children's Panel
members:

        Housemaster: One reason Dalmore is so stable just
                     now is because of two particular boys
                     who continue to stay of their own
                     free will.
        Head: They've had a lot of support, but
                     it's their decision to stay. It's
                     hard to imagine an approved school
                     where one-fifth of the boys have
                     decided to stay but that's what
                     we've got here.
        Researcher: How easy did they find it to decide?
        Head: Those two we mentioned found it
                     very easy. But others are con-
                     stantly chopping and changing their
                     minds. Sometimes I have to be angry
                     and tell them they may as well go,
                     but usually they end up deciding to
                     stay. Sometimes it's the best thing

                              127

to let them go.

Given this philosophy, it is understandable that when
the school leaving age was raised to sixteen there was
much consternation among staff as to how they and their
boys were going to manage. It had been relatively easy
to ask a boy to stay on three or four months until he
was fifteen, but few boys would be willing to stay on
a year and three months or more. The working solution
arrived at was to stop presenting new boys with the idea
that they deserve to get out after six months. If boys
do not expect to be out until after a year or so then
it is hoped the length of time for which they stay on
'voluntarily' will be that much shorter and more
bearable.

Before the raising of the school leaving age, boys
who were approaching their six months and grade five
expected to get released. How, then, did staff
persuade them to stay on if, as they claim, it is to be
the boys' own decision? Several tactics were and still
are used. One is to sow the seeds of the idea of staying on throughout the boy's stay - when he is admitted
or during a group counselling session in which the
group is discussing the decision of another boy to
stay on. But this alone is not nearly enough. In
grade five and nearing six months, boys come knocking
on the headmaster's or their social worker's door to
ask for a licence date. At this point, staff often try
to persuade the boy that going back to secondary
school will present difficulties for him. For example:

Boy: Sir, I've come to see about my licence date.
Head: Well, let me see. Fifth grade, six months
      at the end of this month. But you're not
      fifteen for another ten months...(to another
      member of staff)...Can I see the school
      record?....(this is brought)...See, you've
      got one hell of a school record.
Boy: I think it'll be all right this time.
Head: Why do you think that?
Boy: I've learnt my lesson, sir.
Head: Oh, how's that? In just six months here?

Can you tell me how, when you were in that
other approved school for sixteen months and
look what happened at school after you came
out of there.

Another tactic is to say that if he stays on at
Dalmore he will be able to get leave every weekend and
that really it will be rather like coming to Dalmore
rather than his ordinary school for his schooling.
This is often presented to the boys from the local
town who may go home every evening. Other baits such
as going to stay in the Cottage may also be held out.

There are additional optional tactics available. One
is to say that the boy need not commit himself to staying on the full period but can stay on just so long as
he wants to and that if he wants to change his mind
after a few months he can do so and return to outside
school. This is said in the knowledge that it is
usually easier to repersuade him should he change his
mind as the length of time he would have to stay on to
reach school leaving age would be correspondingly
shorter then. This is sometimes referred to by staff
as 'stringing him out'.

Another tactic is to threaten that if the boy were
released and then 'broke down', i.e. got into further
trouble, Dalmore would not have him back. That is, he
would have to go to a senior List D school, a fate
which boys commonly believe, and are encouraged by
staff to believe, is worse than being in Dalmore.

This combination of tactics, of giving the boy
'insight' into his situation on release and proferring
a set of rewards and threats, usually results in the
boy staying on. Whether the boy himself experiences it
as a free decision is debateable and this I discuss
later.

4.   RECENT BEHAVIOUR

Some boys do not get released even though they have

129

been in six months, reached grade five and attained
school leaving age. One reason can be that recently,
while on home leave or while absconding, they have
committed further offences which have come to the
notice of the police or the Reporter to the Children's
Panel. Recent instances of bad behaviour within Dalmore, however, do not usually lead to unanimous agreement by staff that release should be delayed.

Indeed, behaviour in Dalmore that is construed as
very bad is, for a grade five boy, more likely to
hasten than delay his release since an effective way of
quietening the school down at times of stress is to
release a hardened troublemaker. Staff may feel that,
although maybe not positively helping the boy himself,
release will not do him any harm and will certainly
help the other boys. They may feel that he has shown
as much improvement as is likely, indeed that he is
deteriorating now and is likely to further if he stays
at Dalmore. They may feel there is no more they can
do for him, that although his behaviour is bad, it is
'not bad for him'. The boy is not 'ready' for release
in any positive sense, but if they feel he will never
be ready, he may as well go now as later. If he
'breaks down' after release and gets sent to senior
school, Borstal or Young Offenders Institution, this
may do him good; it may be he needs the strict discipline of such places rather than the therapeutic atmosphere of Dalmore, and the sooner the authorities hammer
him by sending him to a stricter place the better it
will be for him. The following comments from a lengthy
discussion of a boy at one gradings meeting illustrate
some of these feelings:

- Came in eight months ago, this is his fourth
  month in five, he'll be fifteen in four months.
- I think he's got to go. I don't think we've
  achieved anything.
- He tries hard but little progress.
- Isn't this the boy who came to us illiterate?
- More or less still is......

- He's a real hard man. You know, he won't be

free for long. I just don't know what to do with a boy like this.
- Maybe he'd be better in a senior school....

- I recommend release now, but I couldn't possibly predict success and if there wasn't success we couldn't take him back.
- That's fair enough. We can't do more. We've taken him off the streets. We've got him away from the public....he's going to break down before he's fifteen, but maybe that's necessary so long as there's a senior school that would fit him...we got to consider the other ninety odd children here, you know....

A boy's behaviour is not routinely used by Dalmore staff as a criterion for deciding on release. It is only if there is agreement that it is obviously bad that it affects the release decision. The criteria routinely used are the easily operable ones of length of stay, grade, and age. However, the boy's behaviour is routinely appealed to in written reports recommending release to Review Hearings. Insofar as Panels take note of Dalmore's recommendations, and they usually do, then the depiction of the boy's behaviour in the report may influence release. Even if the decision to release the boy is usually made on the basis of length of stay, grade and age, the writer of the report feels that he must document in his report to the Hearing that there has been some progress with the boy. Progress in the home situation may not be known about so there is only the boy's performance in Dalmore to write about, and even if home circumstances are reported on it is still reasonable to feel that a Children's Panel that has sent a boy to a List D school for a year or so should want to know how he is getting on there before they release him to the public to whom they are responsible. If the Panel are to be convinced that the boy should be released they should know that his behaviour in Dalmore is either good or improving.

That Review reports from Dalmore are slanted towards creating an impression of improving behaviour rather

than an 'objective' statement of how they see the boy
is clear from later reports requested of Dalmore when
a boy gets into further trouble after release. These
often portray the boy in such a damning light as would
never have succeeded in getting him released had he
been so portrayed in the Review Hearing. For example,
what Panel would have released a boy had he been described in these terms, as he was some months later?

> Throughout the fourteen months he was at Dalmore,
> little or no change or improvement was noted in
> his general attitude or behavioural patterns.
> Severely regressed boy. Emotionally, his dis-
> turbed and disturbing behaviour was constantly
> being manifested in bullying provocative behaviour,
> dishonesties in and out of school, and a non-stop
> barrage of complaints about bullying by boys,
> allegations of unfair treatment by staff. The
> fact that he was above all an incorrigible liar
> made such complaints all the more time-consuming.

How, then, are Review reports written? Their structure usually takes one of two forms, each of which takes
as its central theme the boy's behaviour in the school,
or correlates such as his 'attitudes' and 'character'.

This first type of report metaphorically glues together extracts from teachers' and instructors' monthly
reports to give an impression of progress. The monthly
reports are usually kept in the boy's file, so the
Review report writer may have before him, say, half-a-
dozen of them. These monthly reports may receive relatively little editing and form half or more of the
total length of the Review report. The following is
typical:

> ...At a recent meeting of staff on gradings, it
> was felt that because of his outstanding progress
> in school he should be considered for release at
> the end of the month. All members of staff
> agree that.... (from this point till the last
> sentence the report quotes, verbatim, extracts
> from monthly reports of three and five months

previously, as follows:) ....He has been a first
class worker, totally reliable and barely requiring
even mild correction. He is well accepted by his
peers; although he appeared to be greatly
disturbed by the loss of his father he is slowly
coming to terms with the domestic set-up. He
is a very decent lad who may do very well. His
high standards of behaviour seem to be much more
than superficial conformity. In view of this
lad's performance it has been decided to write
the report and ask for a Review Hearing to be
convened.

This report does not mention that the 'coming to terms
with the loss of his father' was noted five months
previously (the boy had only been in six months); the
main plank to the argument that the boy be released is
his 'high standards of behaviour'. This report is
typical of the way in which extracts from monthly
reports are picked out to portray progress. Good
points recorded near the beginning of a boy's stay may
be referred to as though they happened yesterday, and
bad points recorded more recently may be ignored
altogether. Monthly reports, although often disputed
by social work staff when presented in the grading
meeting, are objectified as a factual record by those
same staff when they include them in Review reports.
As Zimmerman (1969:354) noted in a welfare agency:

> ....documents often had an obvious character.
> They were seen by personnel as obviously
> factual reports.

Thus, the terms in which the monthly reports are
written become the terms in which the Review report is
written. The monthly reports are structured by four
headings which concern a boy's response to aspects of
the school - 1) work; 2) correction; 3) other boys;
and 4) his character. These are all categories which
derive from the boy's behaviour in the school which
may then be reworked into a concept such as 'attitude'
or 'character'.

One way, for example, in which 'character' may be
deduced from behaviour is through the concept of
'merely conforming'. The report quoted above said:
'His high standards of behaviour seem to be much more
than superficial conformity'. This implies a distinction made by the writer between good behaviour in which
the person puts his whole self, and good behaviour
which is a front, a presentation of self from which he
is suspected to distance himself. Staff require, then,
good behaviour which is not a response aimed at release
but which is a true expression of the boy's 'character'.
Staff usually 'know' good behaviour is really only
'superficial conformity' when they are aware of other
behaviour which is inconsistent with what they see as
the intended front. In a total institution the inmate
who expresses distance in private from his public roles
may find these private actions somehow or other come to
the attention of staff (Goffman 1968).

This style of constructing Review reports by piecing
together monthly reports tends to be favoured by
writers who do not feel they know a boy very well, or
who do not feel competent at writing extended prose,
and so tend to rely on the writings of others. Other
staff tend to use their own observations of the boy,
and in so doing often selectively refer to his most
recent behaviour. This second type of report argues
that the performance of the last month or so indicates
that the boy has made sufficient progress to merit
release. Earlier reports may be referred to, but
usually as evidence of the boy's originally less
advanced state.

A common argument in this type of report is that a
boy has made a dramatic improvement recently on moving
from classrooms to a work situation in Dalmore because
of his reaching school leaving age. It could, of
course, be argued that had he always been in a work
situation he would have been in an 'improved' state
right from the start of his stay, and that his actual
'improvement' is due not so much to progress in the
boy as to a normal response to an administrative
change, but Review reports usually stick to the

'progress' argument. The following report is notable
for being more aware than any other I found of the way
in which changed circumstances have contributed to the
change in the boy, yet even here the boy is given
credit for the change. The changed circumstances
enabled him to 'express himself better', enabled his
true self to be seen:

> All the early reports from staff indicated a
> slow purposeful boy who, given sufficient time
> and the right circumstances, could do well. He
> was just another boy, neither very good nor very
> bad, one who was content to go along with things
> rather than make decisions for himself. The big
> change took place when he was placed in a work
> situation, gone were the pressures and frust-
> ration of the classroom and instead the relaxed
> situation where he could express himself better.
> From this time on, he really progressed, he
> became more confident in dealing with adults,
> and his cheery disposition, willingness to work
> and participate in school matters greatly
> impressed all who came in contact with him.

In both these types of Review report the main argument appears to be that of documenting an improvement
in the boy's 'behaviour', 'attitudes' and 'character'
which therefore merits release. This argument is often
made explicit, as one writer was in the habit of
stating:

> It is our practice to release boys in six months
> time if their behaviour and progress merit this.

Discussions in Dalmore before the reports are written
appeal to the other considerations described in this
chapter, but the reports themselves - the official
notice to the Children's Hearing as the formal decision
-maker - rest heavily on documenting improvement in
the boys' behaviour.

5. PROBLEMS

The other reason that grade five boys who have been in
six months may not get released is that serious
'problems' are perceived to exist. When senior staff
are talking to outsiders about release, they emphasise
the importance of a boy's 'problems', especially those
at home, being resolved. They say a boy is released
when he is 'ready' to go; 'readiness' has two basic
components - his performance in the school and his
situation outside. They say his behaviour inside is
the most immediate material to be worked on, but
ultimately the situation outside and the 'problems'
associated with it are more important:

> If you run a community such as Dalmore and you
> involve the children in their own affairs you
> establish the kind of relationship through which
> it is easy for a child to settle. There's a
> calming influence about it....Now, as a result
> of this, children do very much better than they
> would in other circumstances and so are ready for
> going home very much quicker. So, indeed, what
> has happened is that we have tended to have more
> and more boys who are ready to go home quicker.
> Now, this is the problem because their homes
> are not always ready for them. It is difficult
> because a child's behaviour and the conditions
> he would have to go back to don't always match
> up. People used to think that because children
> are doing fine in the school and it's time for
> them to go back into the community that they
> should just automatically settle in. The bloody
> problems are still there (i.e. those that led
> to their getting into trouble). They have still
> got to face them, maybe even in a more virulent
> form. And they have got to examine them when
> they have time to look at them, not when they go
> back and it's right in their lap. (headmaster)

This situation of the continuing existence of 'problems'
outside despite the readiness of a boy for release on
institutional criteria is partly produced by the

grading system with its philosophy of getting most boys
through the grades quickly. A boy may attain grade
five, and be expecting to be released, and yet staff
do not consider him 'ready' for release (Brooks 1972:
35). One boy even won the annual prize (on nominations
from boys) for being the best boy in the school and yet
the headmaster said at a grading meeting:

> He's gone 1-2-3-4-5 through the grades, but I
> don't think he's ready to go yet.

This difficulty that staff get themselves into indicates a difference between staff and boy's perceptions
of normal passage through the grades. Both staff and
boys see 1-2-3-4-5-release as the norm but, for certain
boys, staff see 1-2-3-4-5 as the normal with release
coming at an indeterminate time later. Thus, several
boys become increasingly anxious when the negotiations
for a release date get, to them, unexpectedly and maybe
inexplicably delayed.

In what ways in practice do considerations of boys'
'problems' enter into decisions about release? A boy's
situation outside Dalmore only becomes particularly
pertinent when he becomes 'ready' to go back to it.
Despite the headmaster's statement above that boys
should be faced with the 'problems' of release some
time before release, staff often do not openly discuss
these 'problems' among themselves until release is
imminent. In monthly assessment meetings it is often
only when boys reach grade five that discussion begins
to focus on boys' families rather than on their behaviour in Dalmore. It is only when return home is imminent that dealing with problems at home becomes urgent.

'Problems' at home often are only considered after a
boy has shown he can behave. This is illustrated by
one letter to a local social work department; the boy
deserves to go home because of his performance in Dalmore, and it is only then that they check to see that
all's well outside:

He has been with us eight months. At a recent

137

assessment meeting (gradings) it was agreed he
had made sufficient progress to warrant consideration for returning to his home. If you are of the
same opinion in respect of his performance at
home, it would be appreciated if you were to
make the necessary arrangements to appear before
the Children's Panel.

By this reasoning, a boy's behaviour inside Dalmore has
to be satisfactory before his 'problems' outside are
considered. Indeed, there were three boys out of the
fifty files I studied in which, after mention of difficulties at home in the original social enquiry report,
there was no further mention of this till <u>after</u> Dalmore
had decided the date on which the boy should be
released. The home situation appears as an after-
thought.

It is when staff ask the question, 'Can we let this
boy go?', that they ask as subsidiary questions, 'Can
we let him go <u>back</u> - to his family, to school/employ-
ment, to his local town, to his peer group?' The
question of the peer group, of the boy returning to the
same group of pals with whom he got into trouble, is
one which is not used to delay a boy's release. There
may be some discussion with the boy as to how he is
going to keep out of trouble given that his pals have
all been in trouble, but there is little else Dalmore
can do to change things.

Neither is lack of employment a consideration used to
stop release. Boys are often sent home on extended
leave to find work and as soon as they have done so
they are released.

The question of whether the local community wants the
boy back is sometimes pertinent to release. Especially
with regard to a small rural community which may have
been morally outraged by the offence for which a boy
got sent away, staff may predict feelings will run high
if he is released after only six months and they may
consider it unfair on both the community and the boy to
release him so soon.

However, it is not going back to the peer group, to unemployment or to the local community, but back to school and back to the family that are the most important considerations for release, as discussed earlier. But if discussion of 'problems' at home is common among staff discussing a boy for whom they are considering release, it is rare to find a Review report for the Children's Panel which reflects this. Review reports tend to be structured around the boy's 'progress' in Dalmore rather than on his situation outside. Few Review reports take up the dominant theme of family pathology adopted in the social enquiry reports that accompanied each boy to Dalmore. Why is this? One possibility is that the kind of family problems that could be raised are usually far from being solved and to raise them in the Review report would hinder rather than help release. Sending a boy out to alternative accommodation is rarely possible and most Dalmore boys have to go back to their parental homes, and this is typical of approved schools (HMSO 1972:Table 13). Staff assume Children's Panels share the theory that bad homes breed delinquency and so, whereas to get a boy sent away from home the social enquiry report may well emphasise family pathology, to get a boy sent home Dalmore may have to minimise family pathology. The difficulty for staff is that they may not feel the home is changing at all, and here the words of the headmaster are often echoed by the other senior staff:

> Think about homes. What can you do to change a home? Nothing. You get the social work departments working with homes. I don't know what they are doing. I don't think they know what they are doing. Certainly not changing them. The basic feelings and attitudes and so on in the home are still going to be there anyway. The living conditions will change very, very little if at all. So when you send him back, you know in many cases that he is going to have to deal with situations that would be very difficult for a well-adjusted adult. In these circumstances he could break down.

Although discussions of such difficulties for a boy may
be discussed at length by staff, it will not get him
released if they put this all down in the Review
report. The way in which family pathology may be
played down in Review reports is similar to the way I
depicted bad behaviour is played down. To take the
example of Johnny - a year after his release, when
asked for a report by a court following further
trouble, Dalmore portrayed the family about as poorly
as possible:

> Family - inadequate. Father alleged to be
> addicted to drink and considerable parental
> disharmony existed. Correspondence with the
> son was infrequent and erratic. Family were
> evicted from their home during the lad's stay.
> Lack of parental interest and an emotional
> climate within the home.

Such a report might be enough to get the boy sent to a
senior approved school or Borstal, but it could hardly
have been written a year earlier when Dalmore had
wanted to send the boy back to his home. The Review
report recommending release, although not portraying
sweetness and honey at home, suggested that difficulties were only sporadic and that things were improving
in that the boy was growing to cope with home:

> Johnny's behaviour continually fluctuated
> according to the prevailing home conditions at
> that moment of time. Yet there is taking place
> a greater tolerance of these conditions. During
> the period when home conditions were favourable
> and the family appeared settled, Johnny displayed
> an emotional maturation in that he was a helpful,
> agreeable, hard-working lad. Only on the advent
> of a home crisis did Johnny's control diminish and
> he reverted to immature, unhelpful, unco-operative
> behaviour.

Thus, although the report goes on to say,

> It is to us therefore obvious that Johnny's

> problem is in his home and that anti-social
> acts are a direct result of unsatisfactory home
> conditions....

the edge has been sufficiently taken off this to imply
that release to the home is not totally out of the
question.

Review reports then are generally based on a boy's
behaviour, possibly refracted through summary concepts
such as 'character' or 'attitudes'. Reports which are
structured around the emergence and solution of a
'problem' are rare, although several mention 'a
problem' in passing. The word 'problem' is frequently
used in Review and progress reports, but usually the
usage is very vague and it is not specified what the
problems are:

> He has matured a great deal and can now converse
> quite freely with adults. This I feel can be
> the determining factor on his return to society
> as he can now approach and speak to adults about
> problems.

THE PRIORITY OF EACH GROUND FOR RELEASE

I have argued that there are five main grounds for
release. There is a tendency for some of these to be
considered by staff and boys before others, and therefore there is a sense in which the earlier criteria
are more indispensable. The first questions routinely
asked are: 'has the boy been in six months and has he
reached grade five?' and then 'has he reached school
leaving age?' Two of these questions - 'has he been
in six months?' and 'has he reached school leaving
age?' - are questions determined by the administrative
considerations of the (former) legal minimum stay in a
List D school, the legal minimum school leaving age,
the boy's date of birth and the school leaving date at
his local authority. The answer to the other question,
'has he reached grade five?' is based largely on his
past behaviour in Dalmore. Thus, the routine grounds

for releasing a boy from Dalmore rest on his good behaviour and on fate or what may be politely called administrative considerations.

There are also two other grounds - 'what is his behaviour like just now?' and 'what problems are there in his situation outside?' These questions are, however, not routinely asked by staff, although the issue of his behaviour routinely structures the reports written for the Review Hearing.

Following the raising of the school leaving age, the target of getting boys out in six months was dropped and this led to an erosion of two of the routine grounds - grade and length of stay. This has left much more to be decided on the basis of the more individualised grounds of 'problems' at home and current behaviour in Dalmore. Consideration of problems outside and behaviour inside comes earlier and more routinely, and persuading the boy to stay on comes later.

THE BOY'S EXPERIENCE OF RELEASE

The most important thing for a boy is that he gets released. A few boys on occasion look on Dalmore as home and would like to stay but they would not say this in the company of other boys since the generally held norm is that everyone wants to go home. As everyone has been compulsorily sent away and cannot discharge themselves at will, the actual day of release assumes major importance.

Consequently, second only to the concern for getting out is a concern for certainty as to the exact date of release. When a boy arrives at Dalmore and is told that, so long as he does OK, he can be out six months to the day, he makes a mental note of the date six months thence, and if he progresses through the grades without hindrance he may take for granted that that date still stands. Although legally incarcerated for an indeterminate sentence, he has the reassurance of the man away for a determinate period. He may note the

142

passage of time towards his date but he does not need to constantly filter information to ascertain when he might be discharged as did Roth's (1963) TB patients.

When he nears six months and grade five, however, doubts may arise. He realises that not all his contemporaries who were admitted around the same time are getting licensed, and that even those that do are not all getting out in six months to the day. Others say they are 'staying on' or 'being kept on' till school leaving age. The most definite action he can take is to go to either the headmaster or his housemaster and 'ask for a licence date'. He wonders how far can he push to know the exact date. One boy, for example, having been told by the headmaster, 'I certainly can't hold you a day over six months the way you're performing now', went back the next week and got this confirmed:

> George: Can you tell me more or less exactly
>   when I'll get licensed?
> Head: More or less about October 19th.

If he is under school leaving age, sooner or later the idea that he might want to stay on is suggested to him. With some boys this may be mentioned at admission or during group counselling, but usually it is not till later that it is made a direct issue which he is specifically asked to 'go away and think about and come back and tell us your decision'. With George, this came a few days before October 19th. George saw me on October 17th:

> Hey, I've got a problem. My housemaster says
> I'll not get licensed this week. I'm fed up
> with this joint, about time I was away.

At this point the man in question came in. There were four or five other boys present, and the following attempt by him to introduce and justify the idea of staying on was for their benefit as well as George's:

> You know, a year or two ago most boys got out

143

in fifteen months, a year if they were lucky.
There was maybe one out in six months but I
sometimes think he was having us on and now
they're all wanting out in six months. I'm
going to work out just how many of my boys have
been in trouble again. I saw some figures said
it was seven out of ten and getting worse.

On the 19th October, another boy mentioned in passing
that the deputy headmaster had included George in a
group of boys to be licensed at the end of the month.
On the 30th October, a Monday, George said to me:

I've got a feeling it could be this Friday;
....(another boy admitted the same day) is
definitely getting licensed. But I'm not sure.
I've asked (secretary and three social workers)
but none of them know.

That Wednesday there was a grading meeting at which it
was decided the housemaster should tackle George
directly with the question of staying on. The next
day, George saw the headmaster and had made his mind
up:

George: I want to go back to outside school.
Head: OK. But you're making a mistake.
George: I don't think so, sir.

Some days later a Review Hearing was arranged for the
1st December and George expected to be licensed then,
which in fact happened, seven months and twelve days
after admission. Out of my sample, George may be categorised as the model inmate, yet even he went through
this usual period of uncertainty near the end of his
stay. If even he became uncertain about the precise
date, how much more do other boys who fear that grounds
may be produced for compulsorily keeping them on,
rather than asking them to stay on. As a rather less
model pupil said to me the day before he got released:

When you come in for six month...when you start
to come in you don't really bother. You just

go on, get home for your weekends. Ken, it's
after your six month you start to worry about
when you're getting licensed.

In addition to being the two most important determinants of release, the criteria of 'doing your six
months' and reaching grade five are objectively measurable and so are attractive to boys whose prime concern
is to know an exact licence date. Indeed, the desire
for certainty is so strong that many boys would prefer
to know for certain a date a month away than be told
vaguely that it could be some time next week. This is
possibly influential in the process of boys deciding to
stay on. In a context of uncertainty the boy is asked
to think about staying on, and one advantage for him
of staying on till he's old enough to leave school may
be that the date is fixed and certain.

Good behaviour is also seen by boys as something
taken into consideration for release. This is often
expressed in the belief that to get licensed you need
to get good reports. It is known that a report is sent
to the Review Hearing and it is believed that this is
made up from reports from teachers, instructors and
other staff. The content of such reports is (accurately) believed to be about one's behaviour. This
belief is fostered by staff who will often tell a boy
who has been in several months but has recently got
into trouble:

We're going to get reports from various staff
at the end of a month to see how you've been
getting on, and whether you get licensed may
depend on them.

The concept often used by the headmaster of release
'when you're ready', if not defined further, is usually
interpreted by boys to mean 'when your behaviour is
OK'.

The extent to which boys perceive problems outside
Dalmore as pertinent to release is difficult to
estimate. Since not wanting to go home for a young

145

teenager may have fairly drastic implications for him, feelings that he would rather not go home may vary from day to day. Something of this ambivalence is shown in the following comments from a sixteen-year old to me at two consecutive lunch-times:

> If I'd come back from leave last weekend,
> (deputy headmaster) says I'd be licensed by now.
> He says it'll be about a month. My probation
> officer is finding somewhere for me to live -
> ken, I had more arguments with my dad on leave.
> I'm not in here for any crime; it's for fighting
> with my dad.

> The probation officer told the school that my
> father wasn't wanting me back. He's a liar.
> The truth is, my dad does want me back. He
> told the probation officer that last Monday.

If such 'problems' were perceived as a normal consideration for release, one would expect there to be considerable negotiation between boys and staff over the implications for release of how such 'problems' were being coped with. In practice, though, most of the bargaining between staff and boys over release dates concerns staying on till school leaving age, that is, the 'problem' on release that boys most frequently accept exists is that of going back to school.

To conclude

Boys in general perceive the same criteria for release, in the same order of priority, that I have described in the analysis in the earlier parts of this chapter. The boys' perception is reinforced by their overwhelming desire for certainty in being told a definite licence date as this means they push for the more routine criteria to be used. Negotiation and bargaining over release is encouraged by staff in order that boys may become more aware of their 'problems' and that, by boys making their feelings known, staff may treat each boy individually. Such bargaining by staff, however, fosters uncertainty in the boy. Boys, by

146

contrast, usually enter into bargaining with staff in order to increase rather than reduce certainty.

In this chapter, I have tried to show that there are five criteria employed by staff and perceived by boys to be relevant for deciding on release. The routinely used criteria - length of stay, grade and age - have to do with administration, chance and good behaviour. The extent to which a boy's problems outside have been solved is not a routine determinant of licence, although staff may talk at length about such problems. It is possible that, following the raising of the school leaving age to sixteen, this pattern is breaking down and that as length of stay and grades become less important so a boy's behaviour inside and his problems outside become more so.

7   Conclusion: "Your problem is you can't behave"

'Begin at the beginning', the King said, 'and
go on till you come to the end: then stop'.
(Lewis Carroll)

SUMMARY

Chapter 2 depicted the way the headmaster and senior
staff describe their work in Dalmore. Their philosophy
emphasises the need of each individual child for help
with his 'emotional problems', 'problems' which are
seen as crucial in the causation of delinquency. Providing such help is defined in this view as the main
task facing staff at Dalmore. Chapter 3 contrasted
with this the main concerns of the boys. While not
denying that they may have such 'emotional problems' or
that staff are aware of the contrasting nature of the
boys' concerns, I argued that the main concerns of the
boys in Dalmore are to do with getting out and that
they perceive good behaviour as the means to this end.
While the staff's official view emphasises the problematic nature of a boy's life <u>prior</u> to his getting into
trouble, the boys tend to take this life for granted
and what they find problematic is how to manage <u>after</u>
getting into trouble.

The tension between these two conflicting views of
what Dalmore is all about has formed the subject matter
of this book. How is each view perpetuated and legitimated in the face of contrary definitions embodied in
the other view? It is important that the non-social
work staff that the boys are in everyday contact with
are less committed to the official philosophy than are
the senior staff, and this reduces the amount of conflicting definitions of the situation that the boy
experiences. It would be tempting to analyse a school

such as Dalmore by arguing that the philosophy of a
reforming headmaster is not implemented because of his
inability to get his lower echelon staff in line and
because of their concern with accomplishing everyday
organisational and non-therapeutic tasks. Such an
analysis does bear some relation to the situation at
Dalmore, but it is far from adequate for there is an
increasing commitment by several middle and lower staff
to the headmaster and his ideas. More importantly, it
is precisely those senior staff who are most committed
to the official philosophy who make the decisions about
leave and release. Since leave and release are the
boys' main concerns, the criteria on which leave and
release are granted are likely to be highly influential
on the boys' view of the school. Thus, although the
senior staff see less of the boys on a day-to-day basis
than do many other staff, it is these senior men that
make the important decisions about boys so it is the
work of senior staff that I have focussed on in my
analysis of the confrontation of official and boys'
definitions of the school.

My approach has been to examine the way in which
senior staff actually formulate boys' 'problems'. How
do they go about diagnosing and treating for each boy
the 'problems' that all boys in Dalmore are presupposed
to have? These 'problems' are said to lie in the boys'
outside environment, especially the home. Chapters 4
and 5 looked at the amount and type of information
filtering through to Dalmore about the boys' home
environments and I concluded that such information is
inadequate for the routine formulation of each boy's
'problems'. Indeed, such a conclusion is frequently
heard from senior staff themselves and the reasons they
give for the inadequacy of such information are the
recent reorganisation of social work departments and
the poor channels of communication between these and
List D schools.

In the absence of adequate information from outside,
staff have only the boys' behaviour in Dalmore to go
on. In Chapter 6 I examined the criteria used to
assess whether a boy is ready for release, and found

149

that these have largely to do with the staff's perception of his behaviour. His 'problems' are referred to
usually only to modify the outcome previously implied
by his behaviour. Problems are discussed, but usually
only when the question of the boy going home has
already been decided.

Routines of dealing with boys on the basis of their
behaviour rather than their 'problems' occur also in
the allocation of home leave. At the weekly meeting
at which senior staff allocate leave, there is only
time to deal with each boy very quickly and so a simple
routine means of allocation is essential. Rather than
individually assessing each boy to see if he 'needs'
it, leave is granted automatically unless a reason can
be produced why a boy should not get leave. Since boys
generally value home leave second only to release, the
loss of leave is inevitably associated with punishment
and so punishment emerges as the main reason for with-
holding leave. There are also pressures from agencies
outside who are unhappy about a boy home on leave and
roaming the streets if he has committed an offence
while on leave the week before. As boys value leave
so highly, a leave system based like this on good
behaviour potently reinforces their view that Dalmore
is all about the correction of behaviour rather than
the treatment of individual problems.

THE LACK OF ROUTINE PROCEDURES FOR FORMULATING
'PROBLEMS'

The lack of routine procedures for formulating boys'
'problems' distinguishes Dalmore from some other therapeutic organisations which produce formal 'treatment
plans' (Gill 1974) or 'training plans' (Bottoms and
McClintock 1973) for every boy in the first few weeks
of his stay. Dover Borstal made such routines central
(Bottoms and McClintock 1973:132):

> ...(i) the establishment of detailed individual
> case history files; (ii) the introduction of a
> basic diagnostic 'training plan' for each

individual; (iii) the implementation of these diagnoses by programs of individual discussion, directed group discussion (etc.....) and (iv) the development of special machinery for reviewing and assessing individual cases.

Apart from (iv) which is matched by the monthly grading meeting at Dalmore, these routine procedures do not exist at Dalmore. This is intentional in that the headmaster wanted to erode the rigidity of a house system in which each boy is assigned a treatment plan, a house and a housemaster to implement that plan. Rather, flexibility and shared responsibility by all (boys as well as staff) for helping with the problems of all is the aim at Dalmore.

However, even in schools where therapeutic and diagnostic routines exist, there is still a tendency for 'organisational goals' to be given priority over 'treatment goals' (Millham et al. 1975). Getting the inmates fed and exercised and amused and safely to bed tend to take precedence over less concrete objectives (Bottoms and McClintock 1973:418). No living arrangement, whether it be prison, List D school, nuclear family or free-thinking commune, can ever free itself from the priority of the routines of daily living together.

In Dalmore, however, it is not just that the organisational constraints of living together take precedence. In addition, there are no routine procedures for formulating boys' 'problems'. Several boys pass through the school such that with no amount of imagination could any reader of their file deduce their 'problem' let alone how they had been 'treated', nor could this be deduced from attendance at grading meetings or other more informal meetings in the Board Room.

School: an exception

The main exception to this is the consideration of return to day school on release (Chapter 6) which boys often describe as a problem. Comments such as 'I hate school', 'I got sent here because I was dodging school' and 'Going back to school – now that is going to be a problem' are frequently heard. Further, staff also define school as a 'problem' in much the same way with statements such as 'He was essentially a school refusal problem' and 'Eddie's problem is truancy'.

However, these two quotes from staff indicate an ambivalence on their part as to quite who has a 'problem'. Whereas the boys are clear that it is they, the boys, who find school a problem, a view shared by staff when espousing the official philosophy, in practice staff alternate between describing boys as having a problem with school – 'Eddie's problem is truancy' – and the school authorities as having a problem with the boy – 'He was essentially a school refusal problem'. The difficulty for staff is that however much they may be formally committed to seeing life from the boy's point of view, they have to cope with the boy's behaviour and they have to work with other authorities such as education, social work and police agencies who have sent the boy to Dalmore precisely because they, the authorities, have had trouble with him. Thus, although staff may sympathise with young Willie who at the age of fourteen has got all he is ever going to get from normal secondary education and feels it would be best if he could leave school now, they cannot act on the basis of such sympathies and have to accept that the education authorities cannot allow him to leave school till he is sixteen. When it comes to deciding whether a boy should be released, the law of the land is a stronger consideration than the perceived needs of the child.

School is the one area where staff begin to define boys' 'problems' in the same way as do the boys themselves, and it is also the one area where there is a routine that this should be considered as a 'problem' for it is always asked of a boy nearing release whether he will be able to cope if he goes back to day school. Yet it is in this area that staff are constrained to define the child as a problem as well as someone who

<u>has</u> a problem, and this betrays their split loyalties.

Bad behaviour as a cue for formulating 'problems'

Truancy 'problems' are just one instance of the normal way in which an individual boy is perceived to have a 'problem'. It is when a boy is perceived to <u>be</u> a problem that it is felt he <u>has</u> a problem. This principle has been stated by a practitioner in another therapeutic school (Spiel 1962:27, quoting Ferdinand Birnbaum): 'A child who makes difficulties suffers from difficulties'. For example, in Chapter 5 I argued that the main way in which leave, when the boy is back home at the supposed locus of his problems, actually leads to the formulation of such problems is when things go wrong and the boy causes trouble at home. It is when he makes problems for parents, police, social workers, etc. while on leave that staff then start working at what problems the boy himself has at home. That misbehaviour is an important device for bringing to the staff's attention boys who might otherwise go unnoticed is illustrated by the frequency with which the following kind of comment is heard at grading meetings:

> There's always a dozen or so boys like this
> going through this school; they cause no bother
> at all and you hardly know they are there.

Using misbehaviour as a cue for formulating 'problems' is to some extent intentional by Dalmore staff. In their view, not all boys' problems can be perceived directly because of the loss of contact with their families and because the problems are so deep-seated that they are rooted in the boys' psyche and are only manifested through bad, or 'acting out', behaviour. However, although misbehaviour may be the main stimulant for the formulation of 'problems', it by no means inevitably acts as a stimulant. In the grading meetings, for example, discussion of misbehaviour often stays on the level of behaviour and the grade is usually derived from the discussion of behaviour rather than any consequent discussion of 'problems'. But even if misbehaviour always did lead to the formulation of

153

'problems' there would be a tension here for staff. For
if all badly behaved boys have problems, then the well-
behaved boys (of whom the senior staff continually
assert there are many) can have no problems - yet the
official philosophy is that all Dalmore boys have
'problems'.

  The ambiguity of quite who has a problem is nicely
shown in a phrase common in social work and psychiatric
circles, namely the phrase 'behaviour problems'. A
child is said to 'have behaviour problems'. Yet it
would seem that it is not the child but adults who have
problems with his behaviour. The child, by contrast,
has problems with adults, and once adults have shown
their disapproval of his behaviour he may have further
problems with adults precisely because they have problems with his behaviour. Only if he then tries to
modify his behaviour to please adults who to him seem
convinced he can't behave can it accurately be said he
has problems with his behaviour.

Language as rhetoric

Usually, then, staff are alerted to the existence of a
boy's 'problems'by his being a problem for adults. If
staff do not then go on to explicate the exact nature
of the boy's problems then the use of a 'problem'
language to describe the boy becomes mere rhetoric, a
way staff talk about their concern with the anti-social
behaviour of the boy without appearing to be traditional disciplinarians. Such non-specific use of the
'problem' language is used every day by senior staff
in conversation and in the writing of reports, as is
shown in three extracts from reports to outside agencies in one boy's file:

  Jimmy was allocated to Bruce House as part
  of the treatment plan.

  Jimmy has made steady progress while at Dalmore.

  It is now time for him to face the next part of
  his treatment and to return home to attend school.

At no stage is it made clear in Jimmy's file what the
'treatment plan' is, how it is related to whatever he
is being 'treated' for, what constitutes 'steady
progress' and in what way return to home and school
also constitutes part of such 'treatment'. As part of
a report on Jimmy this language tells the reader nothing and is meaningless; however, when seen as rhetoric,
as a way of producing a therapeutic image to outside
agencies, it begins to make sense.

So, for example, when the 'problem' is specified, it
is often defined as no more than a statement of an
offence, thus:

- Essentially a school refusal problem.

- His problem has been his failure to return
  from leave.

THE BOYS' USE OF THE LANGUAGE OF THERAPY

It is now possible to see how boys use terms such as
'help', 'treatment' and 'problems'. They do use such
terms, especially in sessions such as Boys' Hearings,
housemeetings and group counselling, although it tends
to be the boys who have been in Dalmore several months
and those who are pro-staff who use this language, and
this suggests they have learned it from staff, either
directly or through other boys. It is not a language
with which they arrive - although doubtless introduced
to it by probation officers and field social workers,
they do not arrive perceiving it as the appropriate
language for use in a List D school nor are they at
first skilled enough in its use to articulate it.

Once learned, how is this language used by boys? Not
surprisingly, it reflects its usage by staff - as a way
of talking about behaviour, and as a rhetoric which
leaves the exact nature of individuals' 'problems'
unspecified.

1. *Behaviour as a problem*

The List D boy does not find it difficult to learn this
particular usage from staff, since for him good behaviour is a very real problem. His main concern is to
get out of Dalmore and he perceives good behaviour as
the way to get out. After having been labelled as
delinquent by various agencies for several years, maybe
feeling fated that whatever he does will be seen as
wrong by the authorities, he experiences good behaviour
as something he has been thoroughly taught by adults
that he cannot manage. For the List D boy, behaving
has indeed become a problem, for return to a normal
life outside depends on it. When staff tell him, as I
have heard them say - 'Your problem is you can't
behave' - the boy is all too ready to concur with this
and to describe his behaviour as a problem for himself.
If he is told, 'Your problem is you can't behave' or
'Your problem is getting on with other people', this is
comprehensible to him, although such a statement may
mean something very different for him from what it does
for staff. To staff who see boys as having 'problems'
which precede their delinquency, such statements refer
to the personality of the boy. To boys who see their
'problems' as following and deriving from their getting
into trouble, such statements refer to the institution
they find themselves in. The language of 'problem-
solving' is sufficiently flexible and ambiguous to
encompass such diverse meanings without the discrepancy
being immediately apparent, and this is crucial for its
continued use by both staff and boys.

2. *'Problems' as rhetoric*

On appropriate occasions, boys who have been in Dalmore
long enough to learn the language of the official
philosophy are capable of speaking it. A typical
example is the following extract from a Boys' Hearing
involving a relatively new boy, David, and a more
experienced boy, Charlie:

> Head: What is it we've got to do with you
>   while you're here, David?

```
David:    Look after us.
Head:     Well, yes, we've got to feed and clothe
          you, we've a responsibility to do that...
          But what else?
David:    Help keep me out of trouble.
Charlie:  We've got to find out his problems.
```

Boys often reiterate the formal rhetoric in this way,
but it is usually unspecified what kind of 'problems'
are being referred to or what 'help' might look like.
A rather pathetic example is provided by a boy who
asked me if he could write about 'My Life in School'
for me. The extract is full of thanks for the way
staff have helped him, yet the only specific form of
help mentioned is the provision of leave. Staff are
liked for playing with him and for the physical contact
involved; he seems to express a feeling of security
but, if so, does not verbalise this explicitly:

Mr.... (social worker)
  He has been very kind to me he all was has
  been very good to me I like him very much
  his mother doesn't stay far away from me it
  is only half a mile.

Mr.... (social worker)
  I like him very much he hits me in the sly
  that i just figured out because he is the
  only one near me.

Mr.... (social worker)
  He has been very good to me he has given me
  fun he resles with me and always takes care
  of me.

Mr.... (janitor)
  He is the one it makes me laugh Every time
  he presses my hand and makes me laugh. It
  is good with him.

Headmaster
  he is the man to see if you have any trouble.
  He has done a trimendis work for the boys and

157

            i thank him very much.

    Mr.... (teacher)
        he has been very good and helped every way
        by keeping the lavs (leaves) in order
        I all so thank him.

    Mr.... (housemaster)
        I like hime very much he helps me out in my
        problems I thank him very much for what he
        did for me.

  The official rhetoric may mean nothing to the boy.
On the other hand it could mean anything and everything.
Gill (1974:73-74) asked the boys in his school, 'How
much would you say your stay at Whitegate is helping
you?', and those who answered 'quite a bit' or 'a lot'
were asked why. Responses covered the complete range
of penal philosophy - trade training, deterrence,
education, training, removal from temptation, improvement of relations with parents, sports offered, social
education, self-insight, punishment. Thus, whether the
language of 'help' and 'problems' means nothing as it
may do to the new boy or more or less anything as it
may do to boys who have learned the language, it
clearly does not mean very much apart from their having
learned the official rhetoric. Thus, when a boy says,
for example,

    Mr X, he's one of the best. Ken, you can talk
    to him about your problems an' that,

it is not at all clear what this might mean to the boy.
I, for one, do not ken what he means.

3.   *The meaning of 'problems'*

When boys use the term 'problems' and do specify what
'problem' they have in mind, they rarely mean what is
meant in the official philosophy. Sometimes they are
referring to their perceived inability to behave,
sometimes to the concerns described in Chapter 3. Boys
do become aware, however, that they are supposed to

have 'problems' at home and so they sometimes refer to
difficulties at home, but such 'problems' at home often
derive from rather than precede their getting into
trouble. For example, one man at a grading meeting
mentioned about the boy under consideration that he
would come to him and say, 'I have a problem, sir', but
the problem referred to was that his father was short
of help in the shop he ran and could the boy get extra
leave to help out. This was only a problem because the
boy was in a List D school and unable to help his
father as he might normally. Another boy who was very
pro-staff and had been in Dalmore a long time described
to me the kinds of 'problems' that Dalmore 'help' one
with. They involved family, employment and absconding,
two of which are problems largely or wholly because
of Ian's residence in a List D school:

> Researcher: Would you say the staff are fair to
> you?
> Ian: Well, they try to help you - with your
> problems and all that. Try to keep
> you out of trouble - help you an'
> that - just understand you.
> Researcher: You say, 'help with your problems' -
> what sort of problems do you mean?
> Ian: If you've got any trouble at home, or
> that. Or perhaps some boys abscond
> and then the staff talk to them an'
> that. And (Cottage housefather), he
> helped me get released a few days
> before the other boys leave school so
> I've a chance to get a job.

The boys, then, although seeing passage through Dalmore as a matter of good behaviour, become increasingly
able to articulate this in terms of 'helping' with
'problems'. But such talk rarely involves a conceptual
change away from the concern to behave and from the
consequences rather than the supposed causes of trouble.
Even if Dalmore is perceived as having helped with
personal problems this is not related by the boys to
their progress within the school and to their getting
out. If the school has 'helped' it is incidental to

159

the main business of being in the school which is to
behave and get out. Thus, a boy who frequently
mentioned to me how the school had helped him to get on
better with his dad, in response to my question -
'What's the best way of keeping in with the staff?'-
said, 'Just doin' as you're told'.

THE LEGITIMATION OF THE OFFICIAL PHILOSOPHY

Given that behaving is a problem for the boys, it is
understandable how they can perceive Dalmore as requiring good behaviour and at the same time employ the
extraodrinarily flexible language of 'problems'. But
it seems difficult to understand how the senior staff
can continue to use and believe in a philosophy of
individualised help when, if my analysis is right,
Dalmore is routinely about something very different.
This is not to say that senior staff believe that they
succeed in formulating and solving all boys' 'problems',
but that they feel that, in a general way, formulating
and solving boys' 'problems' is what Dalmore is basically and routinely all about. I would like to suggest
that certain features of the way in which people at
Dalmore talk enable senior staff to reinterpret the
processing of boys at Dalmore such that their official
philosophy is legitimated rather than discredited (1).

One of these features is that the boys themselves use
the language of 'help' and 'problems'. So long as they
use it in the unspecific way described above, the fact
that they begin to acquire and use this language supp-
orts the belief that they are beginning to see Dalmore
as a therapeutic rather than as a corrective institution. The praise and encouragement social work staff
give to boys when they use this language in public
situations implies that these staff feel the language
entails a shift in perspective which other boys should
learn.

Demonstration of fluency by boys though is, I suspect,
a relatively minor way in which the official philosophy
is legitimated for senior staff. A rather more import-

160

ant self-fulfilling process occurs in the situations in which staff themselves articulate the official philosophy. Two such situations may be identified, although the two may occur together.

One situation is in the monthly assessment meetings and other informal meetings between senior staff in which the progress of boys is discussed. In assessment meetings the length of time taken to discuss individual boys varies enormously; also, quite often the discussion digresses from the case on hand to a discussion of topical issues or to an articulation by the headmaster or other staff of some aspects of the official philosophy. It is in this kind of digression that much of the working out of the philosophy goes on. Now digressions only happen when staff are considering the more exceptional boys. The boy who 'causes no bother at all and you hardly know he is there' does not raise difficult issues prompting staff to digress onto more generalised articulation of official philosophy. The boy, though, whose parents have just disowned him, or who is a confirmed truant yet is still many years under school leaving age, or who has assaulted a member of staff, often perplexes staff as to what should be done and consequently fundamental issues to do with the nature and philosophy of child care are raised. Thus, in grading meetings and other internal discussions among senior staff, the articulation of their philosophy tends to go on in the context of boys who it is manifestly clear to staff have got 'problems'. Articulation of the philosophy then is interactionally grounded not in theory but in honest, perplexed and maybe desperate consideration of real boys. This lends a level of reality to the philosophy since in a sense the philosophy only exists when it is being articulated. To social work staff the philosophy is worked out 'at the mill', 'at the workbench where you get your hands grubby', and the matter of whether it applies to all boys is assumed rather than questioned. Contrary evidence need never come up since in a busy day nobody is going to spend time discussing a boy who presents no 'problems' at all.

The second main situation in which the official philosophy is articulated is with visitors. Senior staff
are here engaged in displaying their school, educating
visitors and arguing with them. One reference point
for them is what goes on in other List D schools, and
it is easier to convince themselves and others that
Dalmore concerns itself with boys' 'problems' rather
than their behaviour if the comparison is with other
List D schools than with the boys' experience of Dalmore. Senior staff proclaim their school as a beacon
in a dark world and against such a dark world the
composition of the flame itself is taken for granted.

Just as in internal discussions of real boys the
discussion may easily shift onto generalised philosophising and back, so in general philosophising with
visitors the discussion usually shifts onto individual
cases and back. Although boys are not routinely
treated at Dalmore on the basis of their 'problems',
there is always a minority of boys who have been so
treated to provide examples for the benefit of visitors.
There is always a case ready to hand to provide an
illustration:

> ....why only yesterday a boy was in this room.
> Now outside Davie was a real thug and made sure
> everyone knew. But if you saw him in here
> yesterday in that seat crying his heart out
> .....etc.

In neither the gradings nor the situation with
visitors is there a requirement to assess whether all
the boys in Dalmore may be adequately understood
according to the treatment model. The actual cases
with which the philosophising are associated are the
most problematic and for practitioners this is adequate
confirmation that philosophy and practice bear some
relation to each other. Thus, whereas boys base their
experience of Dalmore on what routinely happens, senior
staff base their view on what exceptionally happens, on
the more exciting, challenging and therefore exceptional cases. Their philosophy then becomes not a
description of what is, but a program for what could

162

be. Seen in this sense, both the boys and the senior staff's view may be seen as valid for they do not describe the same thing. One depicts actualities, the other possibilities. It is because the staff's hope for possibilities is often presented as an actual description of what goes on at Dalmore that the two views conflict. For staff to believe that their hopes for the future are beginning to work provides a motivation to keep on. So long as this belief persists, exceptional cases may be reinterpreted by staff as evidence that the philosophy is appropriate and operational.

This process of legitimation is, of course, not peculiar to Dalmore or to correctional establishments. It is a normal way in which people-processing organisations legitimate themselves. Thus, in university departments lecturers may only get student feedback from the keen students who come to see them and so the staff may get an untypically optimistic view of the calibre of their teaching and of their students. In hospitals, doctors only go out of their way to discuss the more interesting patients in a way very similar to the Dalmore grading meeting. Freud could generalise from his Viennese middle-class patients to the whole of mankind so long as he continued to see only those highly selected patients. Exceptions to this process of legitimation through selective discussion of clients could only occur in an organisation in which a cross-section of clients is seen, professional-client interactions are always of equal duration and the time allocated for discussion of cases is similarly standardised. I can think of no such organisations.

I do not wish to imply that the senior staff at Dalmore are fooling themselves, are deluded and cannot see what is going on under their noses (as does Becker 1967:242-43). On many occasions they are all too aware of how their school falls short of their ideals. But approved school staff are traditionally pragmatists, men who feel their views derive from years of hard-earned experience. The Dalmore philosophy though is an ideal, an ideal increasingly common today in the child care profession. Perhaps all I am saying is that

163

men who see themselves as pragmatists are, when talking
about their school, a little more idealistic than they
imagine. But maybe idealism in the new community homes
and List D schools is no bad thing.

DEVIANCE AND THE FAMILY PATHOLOGY MODEL

Throughout this book I have drawn a contrast between
the boys' and the staff's conception of what Dalmore is
all about. Whereas the staff see emotional 'problems'
as the cause of the boys getting into trouble and see
the resolution of such 'problems' as the purpose of
Dalmore, the boys themselves see themselves as normal
people and, insofar as they have any problems, these
are likely to have been caused by, rather than the
cause of, their getting into trouble. The staff see
the boys' families as especially important in the
genesis of their 'problems' and of their delinquency,
whereas the boys, whatever they think of and feel for
their families, do not see their family life as having
much to do with the paramount task of getting out of
Dalmore.

  There is, however, one important similarity in the
boys' and staff's models and this has to do with their
use of the idea that bad or deficient people are produced by bad or deficient families, what I call the
model of family pathology. When staff are talking generally, when they are putting forward the official
philosophy, they hold that all or at least most boys in
Dalmore have difficulties at home. And when staff are
talking about delinquent boys they have not yet met,
such as when they are discussing boys on the waiting
list for Dalmore, a similar picture emerges; on the
basis of the Social Enquiry Reports which accompany
applications to Dalmore, staff think that their future
intake is highly afflicted by family pathology. But
when staff talk about specific boys they are in day-to-
day contact with the picture changes. As I have documented, when it comes to the everyday running of the
school and of the routine treatment of boys, staff see
most of them as normal and do not spend much time in

dealing with their family problems, indeed their families virtually disappear from view unless anything out of the ordinary happens such as trouble on leave or unwillingness to go home. Theoretically, Dalmore is full of difficult boys who come from difficult families; practically most of the Dalmore boys most of the time cause staff no bother by their behaviour and resolution of family problems is rarely a practical issue.

This mode of talking about families indicates that family pathology is only invoked as the cause of behaviour which is <u>deviant relative to a given population</u>. When talking about delinquency generally, delinquents are compared to normal law-abiding citizens and so delinquents are defined as a deviant minority whose behaviour needs explaining. Within Dalmore, however, delinquents are not only in the majority, they form the total population for which the staff have responsibility and over which they have control. It would be a totally intolerable working situation were this total population seen as deviant - indeed, by definition, they cannot all be seen as deviant, for deviance, sociologically speaking, is relative to a population (Becker 1963:ch.1). Staff develop an implicit notion of the normal Dalmore boy - a boy who is reasonably well-behaved, straightforward, and tolerably happy. The working day is simplified through developing 'recipes' (Schutz 1964) of action for deal-ing with the standard kinds of situations which emerge with this standard kind of boy. 'Individual treatment' does not happen most of the time; indeed, were it so, staff would very quickly resign for it would entail the abandonment of the recipes which simplify everyday life and enable us to act. This is not to say that treating people as whole and unique persons is not possible, but that there will always be regularities in our social behaviour and group norms will always emerge. Those (e.g. staff) who have to interact with another group (e.g. boys) always explicitly or implicitly recognise these norms to some extent, and base their actions on recipes which are known to work most of the time for most of the group members in most situations. Occas-ionally members act in unpredictable ways, they may be defined as deviant as a result, the recipes may fail, and some explanation may be attempted in order to enable one to act. Thus, in practice, Dalmore staff only apply the family pathology model to a minority of boys, or at least for only a minority of their stay. Family pathology is used to explain deviance, but deviance characterises only a minority of members within any one group.

This practical use of the family pathology model shows a surprising similarity to its use by the boys. As discussed in chapters 3 and 4, the boys use the family pathology model on occasion to explain the behaviour, not of themselves, but of those few of their peers who do not fit in to their world. Boys who act bizarrely, with whom it is difficult to know how to interact, are often seen as 'psyche' or 'mental' (Walter 1975b), and a bad home background is often adduced in order to explain their deviance. Whether or not these few boys are the same few that staff see in terms of family pathology depends on whether or not a boy breaks the normal expectations of both the staff's and of the boys' world. Thus, a boy who can neither cope with the inmate world nor relate to staff could be seen by both parties as having 'problems' at home; likewise a boy who refuses to go home on leave. But a boy who acts purposefully and enjoys confrontations with staff may be seen by them as deviant and hence from a pathological family, but he may have high status with the other boys who have no need to explain what is to them highly esteemed behaviour.

Both boys and staff in practice thus use the family pathology model in the same way - as a means of understanding what is to them deviant behaviour. This is similar to the way others in society use it; police, social workers and other personnel of the welfare state perceive delinquents as a minority, and their deviant minority behaviour is often seen as due to family pathology. Thus, it would seem that it is difficult for people to apply the family pathology model to a total population - only to a minority within a population. When the population is redefined, as when one transfers

from the total society to the mini-society of a residential school, so the nature of deviance is re-defined,
and so the need for explanations is re-defined. The
courts and Children's Hearings send away what they see
as society's deviants, but once away in Dalmore they
form a little society of their own and only a minority
do not fit into that little society.

Boys, staff and others who process delinquents, like
all of us, have conceptions of what constitutes normal
behaviour for a given group and for a given situation.
We do not actively theorise about social behaviour
unless something out of the ordinary happens with which
we cannot cope. We take social interaction for granted
until it breaks down or is unsatisfactory for some
other reason. There may be other reasons than that
another person begins to act deviantly; for example, if
one is profoundly unhappy one is likely to want to work
out what has gone wrong, and to do this one must start
theorising. Many of those we call mentally ill are
profoundly unhappy and consequently they tend to think
deeply about the nature of social relations. Mental
hospitals are perhaps among the few places where the
treatment philosophy can begin to work, for their
inmates often <u>do</u> perceive a need for explaining and
mending the social world in which they live - a need
which Dalmore boys do not usually express. It is not
insignificant that the treatment philosophy has been
formed largely in mental hospitals and in psychiatry
(2). One may be dissatisfied with one's lot for other
reasons, for example if one is in a position of relative powerlessness, has had one's awareness of this
position heightened, and feels it wrong to be in such
a position; in this case too one is likely to want to
change one's lot and, in order to do this, one may
begin theorising about one's lot. Thus the various
liberation movements - black, women's, gay, etc. - show
a degree of theorising about the social relations they
are involved in.

Thus, we can begin theorising for other reasons than
that we perceive someone else to be acting deviantly,
but the perception of deviance remains one important

167

stimulus for theorising. Such theorising need not
involve correct explanations or produce valid understanding - 'deviant' actions such as hijackings and
bombings may provoke, in the media for example, a ser-
ies of explanatory models which militate against understanding such actions (Hall 1970). Deviance can lead
to explanations involving crude stereotypes as well as
deep understanding, and explanations involving family
pathology can be of either variety.

The attraction of the family pathology model

It is worth pausing here to consider why it is that,
when people perceive a boy's behaviour to be deviant
and initially inexplicable, they are prone to adduce
family pathology rather than some other explanation.
Three features of the family are particularly conducive
to family pathology as an explanation when other explanations fail.

Firstly, families are private and their past histor-
ies are even more private. It takes a long time and a
lot of probing to know all there is to know about a
family, and so, when no other explanation fits the
facts, one can always fall back on the family pathology
model for, even if nothing is apparently wrong with the
family concerned, we may suppose that on digging deeper
something will be found. Also, families are very
complex; so if a deviant child's siblings all behave
normally this does not rule out the possibility of the
child's particular history and biography within the
family being different. Thus, one cannot dismiss the
possibility of family pathology just because all the
others in the family do not show adverse effects.

This is very different from other explanatory models.
The main competing models are those which focus on the
school (as the inculcator of middle class ideas incompatible with the life situation of the working class
child), on the neighbourhood, on the adolescent peer
group, and on other agencies (Chapter 2). All of these
groups are more or less public and so more is known
about them. It can be easily ascertained what is the

168

influence on a child of his particular school or
neighbourhood, for schools and neighbourhoods have pre-
existing reputations. Less may be known about peer
groups, but social workers and teachers have some knowledge of these. Agencies - police, social work, etc. -
also have reputations, especially with other agencies.
Thus, it may be easy to dismiss any of these explanations in any one case.

This is facilitated by the belief that the deleter-
ious effects of poor schools, neighbourhoods, peer
groups, and agencies are relatively evenly spread.
Thus, if it is true that a child is being badly affected by his school, people expect there to be other such
children in the school; likewise with neighbourhoods,
peer groups, and agencies. So if there are no or very
few other delinquents in the school, etc., people tend
to rule it out as an explanation of a child's delinquency. As noted above, this contrasts with the way
people perceive families where, even if no other
children in the family have been in trouble, one cannot
rule out the family as an explanation.

Secondly, most families have little power outside the
family group, compared to many other institutions and
agencies. For Dalmore staff to publicly blame a boy's
secondary school, the police in his area, or his social
worker or probation officer would be inexpedient, for
the goodwill of these agencies is necessary for the
continuation of Dalmore's work. These agencies can
fight back. Adolescent peer groups and some local
neighbourhoods cannot fight back and this may make it
easier for them to be blamed. Whole towns, however,
may not be blamed in public as they have some political
power and in certain cases wield financial power over
welfare agencies. Schools, other agencies, and towns
may be blamed in private conversations among Dalmore
staff and models involving schools, agencies, and towns
are part of the philosophy, but it is difficult in
practice to name in writing or in public a particular
school, agency or town as adversely affecting a Dalmore
boy.

In contrast, parents cannot hit back. Their continuing goodwill is not required after their boy has left Dalmore, they are not organised, and they do not wield financial or other power. This is maybe not true of middle class or rural parents; middle class parents can get other professionals such as solicitors and doctors to rally to their defence against allegations of family pathology from a welfare agency and, if one were to allege family pathology in a family in a rural village, the family could maybe rally support from the village to counteract the accusation. Family pathology is usually pinned on urban working class families, for these are unable to organise and repudiate the pinning on them of the blame for their child's deviance.

Thirdly, social work agencies such as Dalmore are mandated to work with families, whereas they have little authority to interfere in schools, neighbourhoods, local adolescent peer groups, or other agencies. Thus, there is always the hope (however distant or improbable) that they can change a family, and this hope gives them a role. Put simply, family pathology gives Dalmore and other social work agencies a job to do. To focus on other explanatory models would either put them out of a job, or would involve imaginative and possibly personally costly reinterpretation of their job (as is happening with social workers who believe in the neighbourhood model and are consequently reinterpreting themselves as community workers).

The importance of an agency's ability to work with a family is supported by the observation that the family pathology model is not used so often with adult offenders. This could be partly due to the fact that social work has fewer rights to work with a family whose offending offspring is no longer their legal responsibility, and also to the belief that the older the offspring the less reversable are the effects of parental pathology. Also, social workers are more likely to be concerned with the children of adult offenders than with their parents. Thus, when the ability of an agency to do anything about family pathology wanes, so does the importance the agency attaches to family pathology in the explanation of deviance.

Concluding remarks

To recapitulate, we usually take the behaviour of others for granted; but when others act deviantly then we may start theorising about their behaviour; when the deviant is an urban, working class child and when all other theories don't fit the facts, there always remains the possibility of family pathology as an explanation.

It thus becomes understandable why so much social science research has focussed on social problems - juvenile delinquency, mental illness, etc. - and why so much of the research on juvenile delinquency has attempted to correlate delinquency with family pathology. The impetus behind such research is the layman's (including the politician's) view that society and social behaviour only needs explaining when it goes wrong. This impetus, though, is inadequate for sociology. Whatever differences the social sciences may have with the natural sciences, they do have one thing at least in common, and that is a transcendence of the layman's view that only the odd and the strange are puzzling and in need of explanation. The social and the natural scientist are committed to puzzling over the normal features of the world, the everyday features of society; these need explaining as much as the bizarre and the strange features. This may put the sociologist at odds with the politician and the practical person who want solutions to their problems, and he may be charged with academicness and irrelevance as a result. He may study what laymen see as problems, indeed he may get funds only for this, but he must refuse to automatically see these problems from the view of those who sponsor him.

This is the approach I have taken in this study. Ultimately funded by the taxpayer, I have looked at what he sees as a problem - juvenile delinquency and what to do with it, approved schools and what to do with them. But I have looked at it in a different way.

171

As mentioned in the Introduction, research into approved schools has been deficient on three grounds. Firstly, it has taken for granted many of society's assumptions about how boys come to be identified as delinquent - it has assumed that the boys in approved schools are there because they have family and other problems; it has not seen the process of becoming labelled 'in need of help with one's problems' as a topic for research. Secondly, it has not seen all parties as worthy of study - it has not found the activities of approved school staff as puzzling as the activities of the boys. Thus, thirdly, studies have not seen the viewpoint of the boys themselves as important, and they have not really seen the boys as conscious, rational human beings; rather, they are seen as malleable objects to be moulded by a regime.

In a sense I am arguing for an extension and trans-formation of the philosophy that boys act deviantly because of their 'problems'. If deviant acts can be explained as an attempt at resolving personal problems, then why may conventional acts not be similarly explained? Most of us, professors, postmen, house-wives, students, whoever we are, have what the treat-ment philosophy calls 'problems' at one time or another and some of us have more problems more of the time than do others. And we solve these problems in different ways; conceivably one person with an infer-iority complex may go out and mug a passer-by to prove he is someone, and another person with an inferiority complex may strive hard to pass his exams and event-ually become a professor or a prime minister in order to solve the same problem - to prove he is someone.

But our personal troubles do not only derive from our individual psychology, but also from our membership of various groups and from our position within society. An extension in this direction of the 'problem-solving' approach could lead to a view of man which is properly sociological, seeing him as acting in pursuit of interests and as basing his actions upon his definition of the situation, and this applies whether we are 'normal' or 'deviant'. It was with this view of man in

172

mind that I directed myself to understanding both staff
and boys as purposeful actors, working to meet their
concerns and actualise their ideals. Only thus can
what is going on inside community homes and List D
schools be properly understood.

NOTES

(1) Some other ways in which approved school staff come
to believe they are fulfilling their therapeutic aims
are suggested by Cornish and Clarke (1975: Appendix 3).

(2) These comments on the theorising activities of the
mentally ill derive from observations made in a
psychiatric unit by Tony Wootton.

Bibliography

Adam, R., Careers in Approved Schools, HMSO, London 1964.

Armstrong, G. and Wilson, M., 'City Politics and Deviancy Amplification', in Taylor, I. and Taylor, L. (eds), Politics and Deviance, Penguin, Harmondsworth 1973.

Aries, P., Centuries of Childhood, Penguin, Harmondsworth 1973.

Becker, H., Outsiders, Free Press, New York 1963.

Becker, H., 'Whose Side are we On?', Social Problems, vol.14, no.3, 1967, pp.239-47.

Blau, P.M., 'Critical Remarks on Weber's Theory of Authority', American Political Science Review, vol. 57, no.2, 1963, pp.305-16.

Blumenstiel, A.D., 'The Sociology of Good Times', in Psathas, G. (ed.), Phenomenological Sociology, Wiley, New York 1973.

Bottoms, A.E. and McClintock, F.H., Criminals Coming of Age, Heinemann, London 1973.

Brooks, R., Bright Delinquents: the Story of a Unique School, National Foundation for Educational Research in England and Wales, 1972.

Carlebach, J., Caring for Children in Trouble, Routledge, London 1970.

Clarke, R.V.G. and Cornish, D.B., The Controlled Trial in Institutional Research, Home Office Research Studies, no.15, HMSO, London 1972.

Cohen, A., Delinquent Boys: the Culture of the Gang, Free Press, New York 1955.

Conrad, J.P., Crime and its Correction, Tavistock, London 1965.

Cornish, D.B. and Clarke, R.V.G., Residential Treatment and its Effects on Delinquency, Home Office Research Studies, no.32, HMSO, London 1975.

Dunlop, A., The Approved School Experience, Home Office Research Studies, no.25, HMSO, London 1975.

Dunlop, A. and McCabe, S., Young Men in Detention

Centres, Routledge, London 1965.

Field, E. et al., Thirteen Year Old Approved School Boys in 1962, Home Office Research Studies, no.11, HMSO, London 1971.

Gill, O., Whitegate: an Approved School in Transition, Liverpool University Press, Liverpool 1974.

Gittins, J., 'Delinquency as Culture', Oxford Review, Feb. 1966, pp.47-56.

Goffman, E., Asylums, Penguin, Harmondsworth 1968.

Goslin, D.A. and Bordier, N., 'Record Keeping in Elementary and Secondary Schools', in Wheeler, S. (ed.), On Record: Files and Dossiers in American Life, Russell Sage, New York 1969.

Hall, S., 'A World at One with Itself', New Society, 18th June 1970, pp.1056-8.

HMSO, Children and Young Persons (Scotland) Act, Edinburgh 1937.

HMSO, Report of the Committee on Children and Young Persons, Scotland (The Kilbrandon Report), Cmnd.2306, Edinburgh 1964.

HMSO, Children in Trouble, Cmnd.3601, London 1968a.

HMSO, Report of the Committee on Local Authority and Allied Personal Social Services (The Seebohm Report), Cmnd.3703, London 1968b.

HMSO, Social Work (Scotland) Act, Edinburgh 1968c.

HMSO, Social Work in Scotland in 1969, Cmnd.4475, Edinburgh 1970.

HMSO, Statistics Relating to Approved Schools, Remand Homes and Attendance Centres in England and Wales for the Year 1970, Cmnd.4879, London 1972.

Home Office Advisory Council on Child Care, Care and Treatment in a Planned Environment, HMSO, London 1970.

Irwin, J., The Felon, Prentice Hall, Englewood Cliffs 1970.

Jones, H., The Approved School: a Theoretical Model, Sociological Review Monograph, no.9, 1965.

Jones, H., 'Organisational and Group Factors in Approved School Training', in Sparks, R.F. and Hood, R.G. (eds), The Residential Treatment of Disturbed and Delinquent Boys, Cropwood Conference, Cambridge 1968.

Macintyre, S., *Single and Pregnant*, Croom Helm, London 1977.

McMichael, P., *Loaningdale Approved School: a Study of the Impact of an Experimental Regime on its Boys*, Godfrey Thomson Unit for Academic Assessment, University of Edinburgh 1972.

Manocchio, A.J. and Dunn, J., *The Time Game: Two Views of a Prison*, Sage, London 1970.

Mason, P., 'The Nature of the Approved School Population and its Implications for Treatment', in Sparks, R.F. and Hood, R.G. (eds), *The Residential Treatment of Disturbed and Delinquent Boys*, Cropwood Conference, Cambridge 1968.

Matza, D., *Delinquency and Drift*, Wiley, New York 1964.

Matza, D., *Becoming Deviant*, Prentice Hall, Englewood Cliffs 1969.

May, D., 'Delinquency Control and the Treatment Model', *Brit. J. of Criminology*, vol.11, no.4, 1972, pp.359-70.

Miller, D.H., 'The Approved School System: a Critique', in Sparks, R.F. and Hood, R.G. (eds), *The Residential Treatment of Disturbed and Delinquent Boys*, Cropwood Conference, Cambridge 1968.

Miller, W., 'Lower Class Culture as a Generating Milieu of Gang Delinquency', *J. of Social Issues*, vol.14, no.1, 1958, pp.5-19.

Millham, S. et al., 'Can we Legislate for Care?', *Special Education*, vol.62, no.4, 1973, pp.10-13.

Millham, S. et al., *After Grace - Teeth: a Survey of Eighteen Approved Schools*, Chaucer Press, London 1975.

Parker, H.J., *View from the Boys*, David and Charles, Newton Abbot 1974.

Parker, T., *The Frying Pan*, Hutchinson, London 1970.

Polsky, H.W., *Cottage Six: the Social System of Delinquent Boys in Residential Treatment*, Russell Sage, New York 1962.

Rose, G., *Schools for Young Offenders*, Tavistock, London 1967.

Roth, J.A., *Timetables*, Bobbs-Merrill, Indianapolis 1963.

Roth, J.A., 'The Right to Quit', *Sociological Review*, vol.21, no.3, 1973, pp.381-96.

Schutz, A., 'The Stranger', in Collected Papers of
    Alfred Schutz: Vol.2, Martinus Nijhoff, The Hague
    1964.
Scottish Education Department, Scottish Social Work
    Statistics 1974, HMSO, Edinburgh 1976.
Simmons, M.M., Making Citizens: a Review of the Aims,
    Methods and Achievements of the Approved Schools in
    England and Wales, HMSO, London 1946.
Smith, G. and Harris, R., 'Ideologies of Need and the
    Organisation of Social Work Departments', Brit. J.
    of Social Work, vol.2, no.1, 1972, pp.27-45.
Social Work Services Group, Children's Hearings, HMSO,
    Edinburgh 1976.
Spiel, O., Discipline Without Punishment, Faber, London
    1962.
Strauss, A.L. et al., Psychiatric Ideologies and
    Institutions, Free Press, New York 1964.
Street, D., Vinter, R.D. and Perrow, C., Organisation
    for Treatment, Free Press, New York 1966.
Sykes, G.M., The Society of Captives, Atheneum, New
    York 1965.
Tannenbaum, F., Crime and the Community, Columbia
    University Press, New York 1938.
Taylor, I., Theories of Action in Juvenile Correctional
    Institutions, paper given to the First Anglo-
    Scandinavian Seminar in Criminology, Oslo, Sept.1971.
Tutt, N., Care or Custody, Darton, Longman and Todd,
    London 1974.
Walter, J.A., Delinquents in a Treatment Situation -
    the Processing of Boys in a List D School, PhD
    thesis, University of Aberdeen 1975a.
Walter, J.A., '"He's Psyche" - Pity or Praise?',
    Community Home Schools Gazette, vol.69, no.6,
    Sept. 1975b.
Walter, J.A., 'A Critique of Sociological Studies of
    Approved Schools', Brit. J. of Criminology, vol.17,
    no.4, 1977.
Wills, W.D., Spare the Child, Penguin, Harmondsworth
    1971.
Words from an East End Gang, The Paint House, Penguin,
    Harmondsworth 1972.
Zimmerman, D.H., 'Record-Keeping and the Intake Process
    in a Public Welfare Agency', in Wheeler, S. (ed.),

<u>On Record</u>, Russell Sage, New York 1969.